FLY FISHING
THE SALT

Also by Al Raychard
from North Country Press

FLY FISHING IN MAINE

TROUT AND SALMON FISHING IN NORTHERN NEW ENGLAND

AL RAYCHARD'S GUIDE TO REMOTE TROUT PONDS IN MAINE

FLYING-IN FOR TROUT

FLY FISHING THE SALT

A Guide to Saltwater Fly Fishing from Maine to the Chesapeake Bay

by AL RAYCHARD

Drawings by Rock J. Agostino

North Country Press
▪ Unity, Maine ▪

Library of Congress Cataloging-in-Publication Data

Raychard, Al
Fly fishing the salt / Al Raychard.
p. cm.
ISBN 0-945980-08-6 (alk. paper) : $8.95
1. Saltwater fly fishing—New England. I. Title
SH456.2.R38 1989
799'.1'6—dc19 89-3084
CIP

 For information write North Country Press, P.O. Box 641, Unity, ME. 04988.

Cover photo by Al Raychard.
A 15 pound Crevalle jack, one of the many species of saltwater fish that can be taken on a fly.

Cover design by Ralph Lizotte.

Book design by Andrea Stark.

Edited by Tom Chamberlain.

Typesetting by Camden Type 'n Graphics, Camden, Maine.

Manufactured in the United States of America by the Maple-Vail Book Mfg. Group; York, Pennsylvania.

10 9 8 7 6 5 4 3 2 1

To the pioneers of saltwater fly fishing.
Many thanks for giving us an exciting new world!

ACKNOWLEDGMENTS

No man is an island, and in that light this book could not have been written without the help and assistance of many people. My sincere thanks to the Maine Department of Inland Fisheries and Wildlife, New Hampshire Fish and Game Department, Massachusetts Division of Fisheries and Wildlife, Connecticut Department of Environmental Protection, Rhode Island Division of Fish and Wildlife, New York State Department of Environmental Conservation, New Jersey Division of Fish, Game and Shellfisheries, Delaware Department of Natural Resources and Environmental Control, and the Maryland Department of Natural Resources for their patience and time supplying much needed information.

Thanks also to L.L. Bean, Inc. of Freeport, Maine, for supplying rods and reels. Their expertise in the field of saltwater fly fishing is greatly appreciated. I would also like to thank Casco Saltwater Flies of Yarmouth, Maine, for supplying countless flies. You may be pleased to know all served well and more than I like to admit are now cruising the Atlantic in the jaws of various uncooperative saltwater gamefish!

I must also thank Rock Agostino of Kennebunk, Maine, who contributed the drawings to this book, and Anne Gorham, also of Kennebunk, for assisting with some of the photographs. Thanks also to Diane Dery of Saco, Maine, who has traveled with me, content to take pictures while I do the hard work—fish!

And finally, my sincere thanks to those brave fishermen who, not so long ago, proved that the salt is not off limits to fly fishing. They opened up a whole new and exciting world and for that, I am forever grateful.

CONTENTS

INTRODUCTION

When most of us think of fly fishing, several visions immediately come to mind: a remote trout pond in Maine with native brook trout rising to the surface at dusk; perhaps a favorite stretch of moving water—on the Kennebago, the upper Connecticut, the Housatonic, Beaverkill, Battenkill or West Branch of the Penobscot—during a caddis or mayfly hatch; or maybe a mental picture of an angler (probably you!) trying to outwit the hard-to-please inhabitants of countless other waters. Add to these "normal" angler visions the dreams of landing powerful Atlantic salmon, or fighting with scrappy largemouth or smallmouth bass, still with fly tackle, and you begin to appreciate the great variety of angling experiences available to you here in the New England and mid-Atlantic States.

Until recently, however, much of the fly fishing fraternity had overlooked one of fly fishing's greatest resources, particularly in New England. It wasn't until the early 1960's when a few dare-to-be-different anglers "discovered" the great Atlantic Ocean and what it has to offer fly fishermen. Other parts of the country with seacoast—particularly Florida, California and the Chesapeake Bay—had long attracted fly fishermen, but acceptance of something new comes slowly in New England. As for now, I can say that accepted it is, and now some of the finest saltwater fly fishing in the country is being experienced from the great expanse of the Chesapeake Bay north to the cooler waters of Maine.

Today, more and more of us are discovering the thousands of miles of coastline from Maine to Maryland, and what they have to offer the fly fisherman. Bluefish, striped bass, bonito, mackerel—these and many other species are waiting; but catching them is an art—as diverse, challenging, demanding, and complex as freshwater fly fishing. Like any other kind of angling, you can't tell the players without a program—and the program can only be obtained through experience. Still, that experience is some fun to get!

It interests me that, although many easterners live within a few hours drive of the coast, relatively few take advantage of that fact and actually challenge "the deep" with a fly rod and line. Maybe it's just too psychological—"if I can't master a stream or a pond, how can I expect to master the Atlantic Ocean?"

The truth of the matter is: you don't have to "master" it to enjoy it. A little basic knowledge is enough for starters, and that's what this book is for: but let experience teach you the rest, gently or otherwise. In the pages to follow, we will discuss needed equipment and how to rig and use it, the species we're after in "the great salt", and likely places to find some of these adversaries. All I am really attempting to do with this book is to show that saltwater fly fishing is practical, affordable, and readily available in New England and the mid-Atlantic states.

Give the saltwater environment a try! You may decide you like some other kind of fishing better—but you won't feel that your efforts were wasted.

Good angling!

Al Raychard
Saco, Maine
January 1989

FLY FISHING THE SALT

Chapter 1

WHY FLY FISH THE SALT?

In a region blessed with fresh water, and with such species as brook trout, brown trout, rainbow trout, landlocked salmon, and largemouth and smallmouth bass readily available, one might ask, "Why do I want to fish salt water?" One might also wonder what makes the anadromous (migrating up rivers from the sea to breed in fresh water) species so special, particularly in view of the fact that the landlocked salmon is a powerful and dynamic individual and the basses are considered this country's most popular angling target. With so much water and such an array of fish to choose from, why go elsewhere?

Well, if you have never cast a fly for striped bass and felt its power on the run, or battled a bluefish, or marveled over the stamina and aerobatics of an Atlantic salmon hooked in a riffle, then I can understand the questions. To explain the feeling of hunting these fish, casting an offering to them, having them accept, and playing them is not easy. Simply said, there is nothing like it in fresh water that most fly fishermen are accustomed to. And while fly fishing the salt or for anadromous fish may not appeal to everyone, it does to me, as it does to a growing number of enthusiasts who are looking for a new challenge and adventure; most fishermen who give it a try do not regret it.

This does not mean to say that those who give fishing the brine a chance will give up on lakes, ponds, rivers, and streams. On the contrary, I am convinced once a trout fisherman, always a trout fisherman. Personally, I still enjoy catching trophy brook trout in Labrador or rainbows in Alaska as much as I do blues in Saco Bay, off Cape Cod, in Chesapeake Bay, or shad in the Merrimack or Connecticut rivers. It's just that saltwater fly fishing opens up a whole new world. A very special world, unlike anything freshwater can offer, and one which can be equally rewarding, one which it makes sense to take advantage of, since so many of us here in New England and the mid-Atlantic region live within proximity of the sea, bay, or tidal river.

Perhaps the easiest way to illustrate the great potential and excitement of fly fishing in salt water is to tell you why it has captivated me, and to show some of the differences between working for freshwater species and those which inhabit the sea or make annual migrations into coastal rivers and streams. Many of the reasons and differences are obvious; others less so. In the end, I think you will agree that there is great potential lying along our coast; whether saltwater fly fishing becomes a full-fledged ambition or just an occasional pastime, it is something worth trying.

FOUR SEASON FISHING

The thing that attracted me to saltwater fly fishing was that it offered an opportunity to work a fly during periods of the year when freshwater action was either not possible or had tapered off due to warming water conditions.

For example, here in Maine where I live, the trout and salmon season doesn't really get started until early or mid-May and even then, water conditions are far from being ideal, particularly in the north country where the spring run-off can keep rivers and streams boiling until early June. There is some good lake and pond fishing, but if you happen to be a moving-water enthusiast like me, little else will do.

By early or mid-May, however, fishermen from Chesapeake Bay north to Cape Cod are already into the blues and striped bass. The season hasn't peaked but some exciting early action is available if you know where to look. When not trolling one of my favorite lakes, I usually head south to take advantage of the ocean fishing off the mid-Atlantic coast.

Two of my favorite anadromous species appear in coastal rivers at this time. Atlantic salmon fishing is at its prime in mid-to-late May and early June before inland rivers recede, and it's difficult *not* to spend time on the Penobscot, Narraguagus, or even the Saco, which passes right by my house.

Shad also migrate in the spring and May is a peak month. Maine has some interesting, yet highly under-publicized and under-utilized shad runs, but the Connecticut, Merrimack, and Delaware rivers are unquestionably the best.

With few exceptions, June and July are the peak freshwater fishing months. August will show some action on remote ponds and in some rivers, but traditionally late July and August are the slowest times for inland angling. On the sea and other saltwater areas, however, things are in high gear. Just about every species which can be caught on a fly are found along the coast from Maine to Chesapeake Bay, offering superlative action at a time when freshwater sport has tapered off on its summer hiatus.

Fall fishing in the salt is good, too. As a matter of fact, fishing for blues and bonito off Cape Cod is often better in September and early October than it is in June and early July. The same is true in New York, New Jersey, Delaware, and Maryland. There are always sea-run browns and coho salmon as well. Freshwater angling at this time of year usually picks up for a short spurt, but in several New England states, the season ends early. Most trout and salmon as well as bass seasons are closed by mid-October.

Fall fishing off the Maine and New Hampshire coasts remains active until mid- or late September, off Cape Cod and points south into October, even November and December; fishing for anadromous trout and coho salmon can provide action well into the early winter months.

In short, saltwater and anadromous fly fishing is possible for a longer period of time each year than freshwater. Trout, freshwater salmon, and bass fishing are good for no more than 4½ months in some areas with peak periods even less. Saltwater and the anadromous species provide steady action for twice that long. For the cost, which at present is minimal except for gear and time, it is an opportunity which can't be beat.

THE ADVERSARIES

Another aspect I greatly enjoy about fly fishing the salt and playing the anadromous species is that they are, on the average, much bigger and more powerful than freshwater counterparts. When I first started fly fishing years ago, I thought nothing compared with a 3 or 4 pound landlocked salmon on the end of a light tippet. I still think the landlock is a noble adversary, but it doesn't quite compare with the bull-like power of a bluefish, or possess the jumping capabilities of a bonito. Either of these fish, as well as most other fish inhabiting the brine or making annual runs, have the ability of stripping four, five, or six times as much line as any freshwater species in New England or mid-Atlantic waters. And when they do so, it is generally with a shocking power that will often astonish the angler.

It is, however, the size of these fish along with their power which keeps me going back. In a freshwater environment these days anything over 3 pounds is worth writing home about, but in the salt, mackerel can run nearly that much, and mackerel are among the smallest saltwater fish taken on a fly. I truly enjoy brook trout, browns and rainbow trout, and landlocked salmon, too. I think black bass are a pure joy on a fly rod. But after catching larger examples in Canada, Alaska, and down south, it's difficult for me to justify a week's fishing trip for 8- to 12-inch brook trout, or browns averaging 1 to 2 pounds, when I can catch fish measured in pounds rather than inches just a few minutes from home or within the same driving distance in the other direction.

I guess what it boils down to is that I have become spoiled over the years. Little freshwater fish do nothing to excite me, unless they happen to be overly selective in a spring creek somewhere. I have come to the point where I want big fish and something that has enough power to give me a toe-to-toe battle. The saltwater and anadromous species fit the bill.

There are also no stocked fish in the salt, obviously. They are as free-bred as anything that lives. Some of the anadromous species like Atlantic salmon, coho salmon, shad, striped bass, and sea-run browns which are now found in a number of our coastal streams are stocked; but because they adapt quickly to a saline environment and the struggle for survival is so rugged, and because they spend so much time in the open sea, they are strong and grow to respectable size. There is little cover available to these fish, not like the cover freshwater species can utilize. Since nearly every creature in the sea feeds on other creatures, only the tough and those which have the ability to swim fast have survived. This is another reason why saltwater and anadromous species hit hard and make considerable long distance runs once hooked.

THE BOUNTIFUL SEA

I also feel that freshwater fishing in many areas is diminishing. Our respective Fish and Wildlife Departments are doing their best to maintain appreciable angling resources, but increasing fishing pressure, changes in the environment, and the increasing threat of acid rain make it an uphill battle. Things simply are not what they used to be, and I fear, as time goes on, except in certain areas and rivers and lakes which are important to the tourist trade, the situation will get progressively worse. Many fishermen today are willing to accept quantity over quality, although I see that slowly changing.

In recent years, we have made impressive progress towards cleaning our rivers and lakes, but many have changed to the point where certain species which need specific habitat requirements, like brook trout and landlocked salmon, can no longer survive. We are rapidly pushing these species back into the remotest of areas or to rivers and lakes protected from development.

Many of our rivers which offer the rapids, riffles, deep pools, and cool, oxygenated water conditions trout and salmon need to survive are being dammed, forming lakes and impoundments in a region blessed with more open water than any other region in the East. We don't need more lakes and ponds. We need to protect the ones we have, and to keep the rivers and streams which are now flowing free from being flooded over. Other problems are threatening our freshwater angling, too. Although I am generally an optimist, I fear that the future does not look bright unless philosophies and people change.

But, in the sea, little has changed. Our striped bass fishery has had its problems, but fishing for them is still good, and new laws and regulations have been made to assure their prosperous future. The populations of mackerel, bluefish, shark, and bonito are strong, in some cases better than ever. The Atlantic salmon, like the striped bass, has its problems, but considering the spirit of this fish and the growing concern and willingness of governments to work together towards rebuilding the resource, I think the salmon will make it. Shad runs typically fluctuate in numbers from year to year, but overall the species is doing well—in fact, is making a comeback to many native rivers along the New England coast. And new resources, such as coho and sea-run brown trout runs are being established. There is, indeed, a great deal to fish for out there.

Along with this, while many freshwater areas are disappearing for one reason or another, rarely is a productive saltwater fishing area lost. As a matter of fact, new ones are being discovered all the time, offering the angler more places to go to practice his craft. And, because of the length of our coastline and the size of our bays and number of rivers entering the sea, there is ample room for everyone.

THE CHALLENGE

There are several other attributes about fly fishing the salt and coastal rivers which really excite me. Productive and consistent fly fishing for both saltwater and anadromous fish often brings out the best hunting instincts in us. You do not have to be a hunter *per se,* but to get within casting range of striped bass holding in a tidal river or grass bed, or a coho or Atlantic salmon stationed at the head of a pool, you actually have to stalk it like a thief in the night. The same is true when fishing from a boat just outside the surf or when you want to fish a school of blues chopping the surface. You have to scout the situation out, approach carefully, and then put all your casting ability to work in order to achieve success. Contrary to common belief, most saltwater fish can be easily spooked, even the larger, more vicious individuals.

Casting into a school of fish, like a cluster of bluefish on a feeding spree, is also something I like. Just the sight of it is enough to get the adrenalin flowing; the excitement and opportunity such a situation affords are truly unique in all of angling. The same is true with bonito or striped bass. The action is fast, successful, and quite often, hectic. In these periods it is possible to catch several fish in a relatively short period of time, and is something you won't soon forget.

As you read this book, you will notice that in following chapters I talk about flies and tackle. No insect life (as freshwater fishermen know it) hatches over the sea and, as mentioned earlier, most saltwater fish feed on other fish, which means two things: exact imitation is not necessary to finding action; and, flies which produce the best results are those used below the surface—streamers and bucktails.

To the novice or inexperienced fly fisherman this can be a major advantage since "matching the hatch" can be quite a dilemma and in the general sense, fishing subsurface flies is often easier and usually produces more action throughout the course of the season. This also makes it easier on the fly-tier. Most saltwater flies are basic and quite easy to construct, although, as you will see in Chapter 3, the philosophy surrounding saltwater offerings is changing to more detailed and imitative designs.

When it comes to the anadromous species, the Atlantic salmon, coho salmon, sea-run trout, and shad, subsurface patterns are best nine times out of ten. Atlantics will take a dry, but the majority are taken below the surface, and the same can be said of coho, sea-run browns, and shad. Except for Atlantic salmon flies, those used for other species are rather basic and easy to tie.

As for tackle, again, you don't need anything special or expensive. Some enthusiasts seem to go for the expensive reels, but if you already fly fish for trout, freshwater salmon, and bass, you have what is needed to get started for most saltwater and anadromous species. One of the most important things to remember is to have sufficient backing and to take care of your equipment. (More on that later.)

Successfully fly fishing for most saltwater fish and the likes of Atlantic salmon, coho salmon, and sea-run browns is not simple. Nor does action come easily or quickly, especially to those who underestimate their prey. These fish and the habitat in which they are found demand respect, tact, special consideration, and techniques which are somewhat unusual and unfamiliar to the typical freshwater fly fisherman. There are obstacles to overcome such as the wind and tides, and other techniques which make this corner of the art different, such as hunting your fish before casting. It can all be reckoned with, however, and once it is understood and appreciated for what it is, saltwater fly fishing and casting a fly to anadromous species is, without a doubt, one of the most exciting and challenging forms of angling available to the fly fisherman.

Chapter 2

THE INSHORE AND ANADROMOUS SPECIES

Saltwater fish are often mentioned in different categories: those fish generally found in deep water or "offshore"; and those which are found in shallower water closer to the coastline or in rivers and bays. These fish are generally referred to as the "inshore" species and include among others, mackerels and members of the sea bass family. It is often difficult to differentiate between the two categories, since just about all saltwater fish are found in both deep water and shallow water at one time or another, depending upon water temperature and food.

For example, some fishermen and writers consider the bluefish offshore fish since they are often found miles out to sea, but I consider them an inshore species in this text. The same is true with the striped bass. Found in rivers and bays when warm water temperatures and adequate forage are available, stripers have been found 20 miles or more out to sea. We will consider them an inshore adversary, too.

Because much of the best fly fishing is found around bays, estuaries, tidal rivers, breakwaters, and within a few miles of the coast, this book will dedicate much of its space to those fish found "inshore". The fish specifically mentioned in this chapter will generally be found in depths ranging from the surface down to about 50 feet, but actively found working the surface. When these fish are found at shallow depths you can often see the result of their feeding frenzy; using floating lines and surface lures or streamers, fishing for them is much more exciting than fishing for offshore, deep water counterparts.

Another type of fish we will mention is "anadromous", those fish which are born in fresh water, then go to sea to mature, returning to a river to spawn. Prime examples are the Atlantic salmon and the shad. Anadromous species are not actually full-fledged ocean inhabitants but, because they do spend a great deal of time in the salt, they offer some excellent fly fishing as they return to the river of their birth, and they can be taken in a saline environment. Because they are so readily available in New England and in several rivers further south, we will offer them in these pages. We will also look at sea-run brook trout and brown trout, since good fisheries have been established in Maine and Massachusetts which offer noteworthy opportunities.

INSHORE SPECIES—THE BIG FOUR: BLUEFISH, BONITO, STRIPED BASS, AND MACKEREL

BLUEFISH ***(Pomatomus saltatrix).*** Of the fish inhabiting our coasts, the bluefish is my favorite. I have caught many, and each is a special experience to be remembered—something making you want more! The bluefish, also called simply "blue" and sometimes referred to as "snapper" or "chopper" in some areas, is a dynamic powerhouse once enticed to the rod; few other fish off our coast are capable of matching its fighting quality.

Several attributes make bluefish prime adversaries for the fly fisherman. First, they are often found in relatively shallow water and rivers, stuffing themselves on baitfish, which means it is often possi-

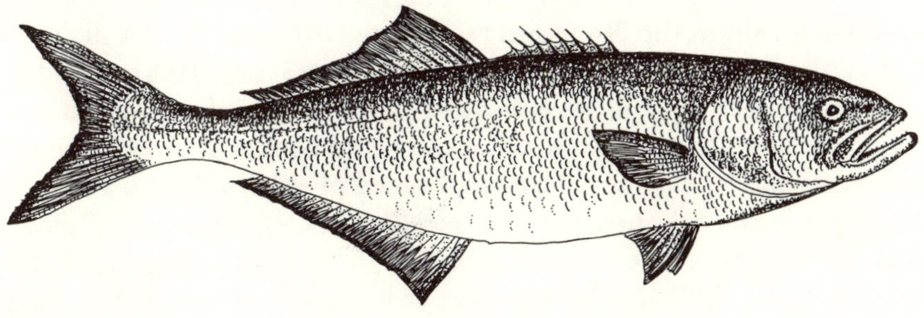

Bluefish — *Pomatomus saltatrix*

ble to cast a fly for them off breakwaters, piers, and wharfs, even by wading when conditions are right. Bluefish prefer water temperatures in the low 60's, and, as long as this temperature range is maintained and adequate food is available, going offshore or into deeper water is not necessary.

Also, bluefish are famous for their savagery. They are often spotted behind a school of pogies or alewives, forcing them to the surface in a frenzy. A good indication that bluefish are in a certain location is when you see a school of baitfish exploding from the surface. When you see this happen, a cast into the madness is almost a sure strike, providing the approach is right. For example, never run your boat into the school; rather, stay off to one side, preferably on the upwind edge, casting into the action. If possible, have the person operating the boat stay on the edge of the frenzy and, often, it will be possible to hook into several blues before the school moves to another location.

Bluefish are always hungry, always willing to wallop a surface popper or streamer with vengeance. When found in deeper waters, they can easily be chummed using cut pogies, alewives, or herring, but because of the blues' insatiable appetite, whether found on the surface or down below, once located, they provide some of the best fly-rodding the New England and mid-Atlantic coasts have to offer.

Bluefish have extremely sharp teeth, capable of cutting a monofilament leader up to the 20-pound test range with ease. If you decide to stick with monoleaders, keep them between 60- and 100-pound test, and cut the leader back several inches after each fish is boated.

I prefer wire leaders, or a piece of plastic-coated wire between fly and monofilament leader. I attach a piece of #3 solid wire to the fly or popper using a Figure 8 Knot (see Chapter 4), forming a Haywire Twist in the other end (see Chapter 4), to which I attach my leader coming off the fly line. The wire leader need not be too long, perhaps 4–5 inches at most.

Another option is to use flies or poppers with a permanent piece of looped wire incorporated as part of the lure. The wire sticks out beyond the eye of the hook about 3–4 inches and eliminates the need for a wire leader. I was introduced to this idea several years ago while fishing for blues off Cape Cod and now tie all my bluefish flies and poppers this way. Unfortunately, the idea hasn't caught on with commercial tiers, and for this reason, the concept is illustrated in Chapter 4 for those of you who tie your own flies.

Whenever bluefish are found working the surface, floating lines are best. They are easier to work with, and they allow you to supply better action to the fly or popper, which is important whenever working for surface-feeding fish. My second choice would be a sink-tip (they are the easiest sinking option to work with) but I often keep a full-sinking line on hand, too. It comes in handy, and is necessary when bluefish are found at deeper depths.

Bluefish are found along the entire New England and mid-Atlantic coastline although their numbers vary greatly. The best action, and the largest concentration of blues, is from the Kennebec River in Maine to down around Cape Cod, off the Connecticut and Rhode Island coasts, and down to Chesapeake Bay, where millions are available each summer. Generally, mid-June through mid-October is the best time to try for blues in southern New England and points south, with July, August, and early September the best time further north. Bluefish run anywhere from 7 to 15 pounds as a rule, with a few up to 20 pounds possible off Massachusetts and points south.

BONITO ***(Sarda sarda).*** The Atlantic bonito is a member of the mackerel family (genus *Sarda*) and, like other mackerels, is found along the New England and mid-Atlantic coasts. Typically, its range extends from Nova Scotia all the way to Argentina, with some of the best fly-rodding along the northeast coast off Massachusetts, Rhode Island, Connecticut and down to Chesapeake Bay. Schools can be found off the Maine and New Hampshire coasts, but the bonito is not a prime target in these areas. One of the fastest fish that swims, the bonito is a marvelously powerful fighter, providing some of the best saltwater action for the fly fisherman.

In some ways, the bonito is still somewhat of a mystery fish to many fly fishermen, especially New Englanders, undoubtedly due to the popularity and availability of the bluefish, striped bass, and mackerel. Unless you happen to fish specifically for the bonito, there is a chance one will never be seen, even though its feeding activity and the methods used to fly fish for it are similar to those for the more popular species. Those who are familiar with the bonito, however, don't seem to mind its obscure existence, with many preferring to keep its presence and fighting expertise a secret.

There are many who probably would not recognize a bonito if they caught one. Outwardly, the bonito is a steel blue or blue-green color along the back, with the lower flanks silvery, a truly aesthetic individual. There are two dorsal fins: the first is long, having between 20–23 spines; the second fin is smaller, having 13–18 rays followed by 7–10 smaller finlets. The anal fin is generally silvery or whitish in color, and is followed by 6–8 finlets tapering back towards the tail, which is large and concave-shaped, much like a tuna. A distinguishing characteristic is that bonito have stripes, generally 7–9 of them, on the back (not on the belly), which run from the middle of the fish in a backwards tapering angle towards the dorsal fins. Inside, bonito have no teeth on the tongue and no swim bladder.

The fly fisherman need not worry about knowing what bonito look like or even where to look for them, although it never hurts. Much of the sport fishing for this individual is done from charter boats out of such places as Falmouth, Massachusetts, on the southern tip of Cape Cod; Newport, Rhode Island; and ports along the Connecticut and mid-Atlantic coasts. These captains are familiar with the bonito, know

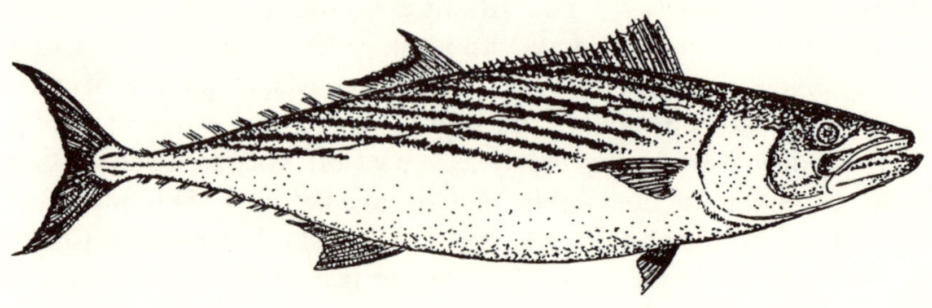

Bonito — *Sarda sarda*

where the best fishing will be found, how to fish for them, and are actually the fly fisherman's best chance for success until some experience is obtained. I have always felt that the cost of a charter boat is almost always worthwhile given the amount of information one can obtain, and I feel this is especially true when it comes to bonito.

Generally, bonito travel along the coast in schools, sometimes coming fairly close to shore, but most often staying 1 to 5 miles out. The times I have fished for them, we seemed to find most action after the 2-mile mark, although there are times when bonito may actually be found off the mouth of a river or large bay. Rarely will bonito enter a bay or estuary unless water temperatures and food give it an occasion to do so; then it becomes necessary to travel some distance before a school is located.

The secret to successful fishing for bonito is being able to recognize an area being utilized as a feeding arena. Bonito are often spotted close to the surface much like bluefish, and the result from their feeding frenzy is basically the same. A major difference in the scenario is that, once a school of bonito has been sighted, it is important to position your boat, and cast *ahead* of the fish, *not* where they are actively feeding. A floating line is best, but keep a rod rigged with a sinking-tip line handy; it is often necessary to get the fly down a few inches.

Also, unlike the bluefish, which seems to prefer rather large flies or poppers when working the surface, bonito are more receptive to patterns less than 4 inches long, with those between 2 and 3 inches bringing the most action. Streamers and bucktails of white polar-bear hair and bucktail and white marabou incorporated with Mylar strips are among the most popular offerings.

The fly fisherman will also find it necessary to experiment before the right retrieve is found whenever bonito are the target. Each situation is different. Some will insist that the fastest retrieve possible is best, making the fly zip through the water, and I have taken bonito this way. On the other hand, I have taken several large bonito with a slow retrieve, and found action when working the fly at any speed in between.

Always remember bonito are strong adversaries and extremely fast swimmers. Once hooked they can easily cover 100 yards or more. Use a light drag, leaders in the 10–12 pound test range, and a reel loaded with plenty of backing. These fish generally range from 4–8 pounds, and with their power and speed, it may feel like the Devil himself is on the end of the line!

STRIPED BASS ***(Morone saxatilis).*** Of all the fish that swim in salt water and are available to Atlantic Coast anglers, the striped bass is probably the best known and most sought after. Found from the St. Lawrence River south to northern Florida, and in the Gulf of Mexico off Florida, Louisiana, and Mississippi, the "striper," as it is often called, has been an important food fish, known to saltwater fishermen since the 1600's. Here in New England, striped bass are a highly important species, from both a commercial and sport fishing perspective.

Even though the striped bass fishery appears to be in trouble, it is difficult not to fish for them. They are such exciting and magnificent game fish it would be like putting a piece of candy in front of a child and saying, "Don't touch." When the stripers "are in", they are simply too much to resist but fortunately, fly fishing is the least damaging form of angling and it is possible to take advantage of their inshore presence without catastrophic harm to the resource or individual fish, providing the fly fisherman's only reward is in successfully catching a striper on a fly and not taking it home for the freezer.

The striped bass is a voracious and opportunistic predator, which means it will always be found where there is an abundant supply of food. In open water of a bay or estuary it will be found anywhere from the surface down to 120 feet, but when inside a river or when found close to shore, which is frequently, striped bass will hang in water less than 30 feet deep. I have found much of my action between the surface and 15 feet in rivers which makes this fish a prime fly fishing target when found in close.

Typically, the striper likes some kind of structure or turbulent water conditions whenever he is not in deep water. Tidal rips, a ledge forming a riffle on the incoming or outgoing tide, on a break where warm water of a river meets the cold water of the sea, and around piers, breakwaters, jetties, and in the surf are all potential hotspots. In fact, any location which puts baitfish at a disadvantage is good.

Fly fishermen will find that the striper can be a frustrating adversary at times. If we were to compare the bluefish with the rambunctious brook trout, most always willing to cooperate once located and with the right fly action, we would have to compare the striper with the brown, often selective, antagonizing even when conditions are right. Many times, the right size fly is a major key to success. Striped bass are big, but this does not mean big flies are the rule, and if you find yourself in a situation where fish are nipping your offerings, a change in size (not necessarily in pattern), can make a big difference. The biggest striper I ever landed weighed just over 20 pounds and was taken on a size 1 standard hook, which is small for saltwater. The point here is not to get trapped in the old philosophy that big flies take big fish. It simply isn't true, particularly when fly fishing the salt. Don't be afraid to experiment.

Also, striped bass seem to have particular times of the day when they are more cooperative. I like to fish for them in the early morning, from just before dawn to 9:00 A.M. or so, until the sun is full up, and then again late in the afternoon, from 5:00 P.M. to just after dusk. At such times bass seem more active and more willing to hit regardless of the tide. At other times, the fly fisherman may have to go to deeper depths and look for some kind of tidal current to provide assistance. If you want a real challenge, night fishing can be excellent.

As a general rule, the fly fisherman should always carry both a floating and sinking or sink-tip fly line whenever working for stripers.

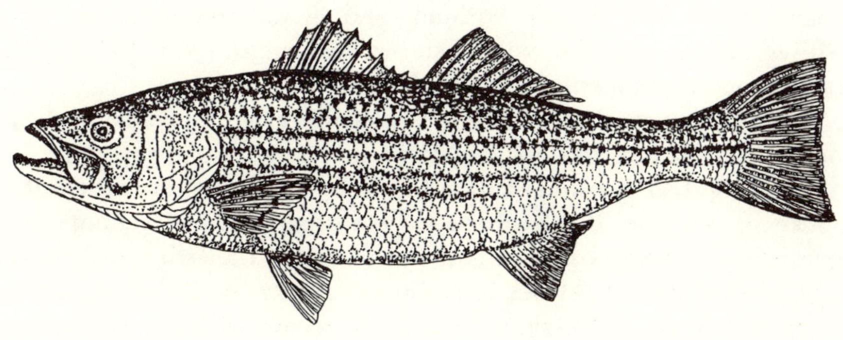

Striped Bass — *Morone saxatilis*

We may prefer fishing the surface, but with the stripers this isn't always possible, making a sinking line a necessity. Leaders can be relatively short, between 4 and 5 feet, and I generally go with straight monofilament in the 12 to 14 pound class. Make sure your reel has plenty of backing (at least 200 yards) and the drag is working properly and set on light. Striped bass are extremely powerful fish and, most assuredly, will take your fly for a ride.

Unfortunately, the East Coast striped bass fishery appears to be in trouble, with a noticeable drop in numbers and size of fish in many areas. Formerly, bass were known to reach weights exceeding 120 pounds, and numbered into the millions. Today, due to several factors (such as overfishing on the commercial end, but also due to an increasing demand from sport-fishermen, pollution, chemical contamination, and herbicides, particularly in vital spawning areas, such as in and around Chesapeake Bay), the resource has been reduced substantially and may never recover to its historical abundance. Currently, stripers in the 5 to 15 pound class are the average, with many taken of heavier weight. Although most states along the East Coast do see annual migrations each summer, they are not as predictable, nor are their numbers as big as in former years. Some states, in fact, now impose special length limits, as well as bag limits, on striped bass. Make sure you are familiar with any and all state regulations.

It will, of course, take more than bag and length limits to bring the striper back. Sport fishermen can help by releasing any striped bass they catch; like most freshwater fish, stripers can be released easily and without danger to both fish and fisherman if done properly.

When the fish is brought to the boat or shore, try to release it as quickly as possible. If it happens to be a small bass—a "schoolie"—a fly can be worked loose relatively easily while the fish is still in the water. But if the fly refuses to come out gently, hold the fish with a wet towel, rag, or tee-shirt, and using a pair of long-nose pliers, dislodge the fly. If the fly has been taken deep, it might be best to cut the leader as close to the hook as possible. Place the bass back into the water in its natural swimming position and move it in a back and forth motion until enough strength has been regained so it can swim away under its own power. Depending upon how tired the fish is, the procedure only takes a matter of minutes. Release any fish in shallow water if possible in the event that it has not regained all its power; you can then recapture it if necessary and provide further assistance.

MACKEREL *(Scomber scombus* and *Scomber colias).* There are two mackerels which frequent our inshore coast. The Atlantic mackerel *(Scomber scombus)* is the larger, averaging between 1 and 1½ pounds or 14–18 inches in length. At times, Atlantic mackerel may reach a weight of 2 pounds, but anything over this mark is considered large.

The tinker mackerel (*Scomber colias*), on the other hand, rarely exceeds 8–14 inches in length. A big one will weigh less than one pound, but what it lacks in size it makes up in cooperative spirit and enjoyment of catching. Once a school has been located, it is often possible to hook a dozen or more before the school moves to a new location. They are nothing but pure fun on light fly fishing gear.

Actually, the size difference between these two fish is enough to tell them apart, but for the more observant eye, the Atlantic mackerel has no spots on the sides below the midline nor does he have a swim bladder; the tinker mackerel, or chub mackerel as he is also called,

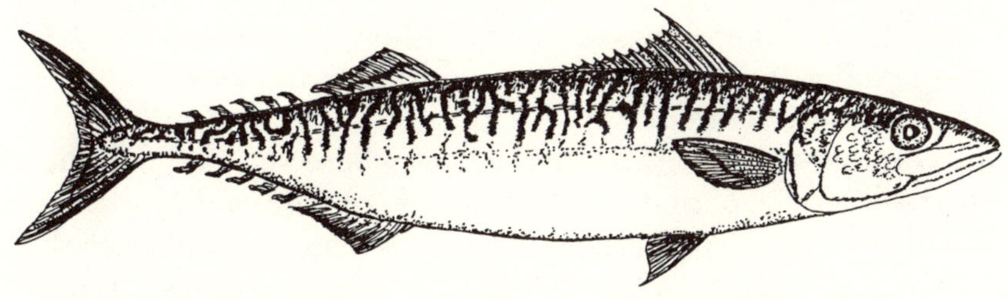

Mackerel — *Scomber scombus; Scomber colias*

possesses both. Both fish have fleshy adipose eyelids, covering the anterior and posterior parts of the eye, and the two dorsal fins are widely separated from each other.

Throughout much of their range, which extends all along the New England coast and as far south as Florida and Brazil, both fish are simply referred to as mackerel, with little concern over the difference between the two. The reason for this may be the simple fact that since both are so readily available and such prolific targets with sport-fishermen, little thought has been given to their individuality except for the difference in size. Another reason may be that in most cases, no one knows for sure which fish will be caught when you go "mackerel fishing", since both share the same waters. To my knowledge no one goes "tinker mackerel" fishing or "Atlantic mackerel" fishing; they simply go "mackerel fishing", which has led many to believe that both fish are the same.

But one thing is for certain, and that is that mackerel are probably the most dependable gamefish found along the New England coast in the summer. Just like clockwork they will start to show up off the Connecticut and Rhode Island coasts in mid-to-late May (if not earlier), and are around Cape Cod at about the same time. Mackerel will be found moving into New Hampshire waters and along the Maine coast south of Casco Bay around the first week of June with areas further east being occupied starting in late June or early July. Generally speaking, mackerel provide active fishing all summer long, often into September in northern waters, with early October being about the limit in areas south of Cape Cod.

Mackerel are school fish, which means where you find one there's an excellent chance of finding hundreds (if not thousands!) working in a general area. In the open regions of a bay, mackerel will often drive schools of smaller baitfish out of the water, but sometimes it is necessary to search for them either by trolling or with electronic fish finders. I prefer to concentrate around lobster buoys, while casting off a rock jetty or maneuvering my boat close to the surf and casting towards shore are good possibilities when mackerel are in close. Mackerel make their presence less known than bluefish and stripers, but once located, some steady action is usually possible.

Whenever found close to shore, in a bay, or hanging around the mouth of a river, mackerel are usually close to the surface, which makes them a good target for the fly fisherman. While a floating line will work whenever fish can be seen, a fast-sinking-tip line or full-sinker offers a better advantage since it is imperative to get your offering down to the fish (perhaps 8 feet) whenever fly fishing the salt. Unlike most freshwater adversaries, most fish in the sea will *not* rise to a lure because food is so abundant and because leaving the protection of the school is dangerous. You must get that fly down to the fish's eye level, and a sinking line of some kind is the best way to go. A good tactic is to troll for them.

Mackerel also have rather small mouths, so flies need not be big. I prefer flies in the 4, 6 and 8 size class, tied slightly thicker than for trout, and generally incorporated with some Mylar or tinsel. Anything that is bright or gives some flash seems to work well.

For its size, mackerel provides a surprising struggle once hooked—nothing spectacular, but enough to keep the rod bouncing. In general, I would have to say there is not much challenge to mackerel, but they are a whole lot of fun, providing steady action once a school has been found. I like to increase the enjoyment by fishing with a couple of dropper flies attached to my leader, much like a Christmas tree rig used with spinning outfits. Two or even three mackerel on the end of a light fly rod kit is a high possibility and much more fun.

There is another mackerel which frequents the southern New England coast, coming as far north as Cape Cod, Connecticut, and Rhode Island. The king mackerel (*Scomberomorus cavalla*) or kingfish, is the largest of American Spanish mackerels, reaching lengths of 5 feet and weights of up to 100 pounds. When caught on a fly they offer a powerfully spectacular display which can be compared to that of the bonito and, in some respects, the bluefish. Most kings average between 7 and 25 pounds.

Like most mackerels, the king is often found close to the surface, but generally stays in deeper waters, coming in close only on occasion. Chumming is a good way of attracting these fish, and when king mackerel finally move into a chum-slick, they can be caught on surface poppers as well as streamers. In most cases, the retrieve for the king must be fast to both attract and hook this individual, making the trolling of streamers a better tactic in almost all cases.

Because of the king mackerel's size and power, heavy fly fishing gear is recommended. A rod of at least 9 feet is suggested, designed for an 8 or 9 weight line with leaders in the 10–20 pound test class, with the larger sizes best. Your reel should carry a minimum of 200 yards of backing and have a proper working drag system. A floating line and fast-sinking line should be carried, since kings are often found down several feet. Some of the best fishing for king mackerel is off Massachusetts, Connecticut, Rhode Island, New York, and especially New Jersey south to and including Chesapeake Bay.

* * *

ADDITIONAL SALTWATER SPECIES: ALBACORE, COBIA, POLLOCK, SAND SHARK, WEAKFISH, SPOTTED SEA TROUT, AND DOLPHIN

Several other species are available to the Atlantic fly fisherman. Although not as popular nor as well known, and less of a prize than the bluefish, striped bass, bonito, and mackerels, they are, nonetheless, readily available and offer an interesting challenge on medium-to-heavy fly gear.

ALBACORE *(Euthynnus alletteratus)*; also Little tunny, False albacore. The little tunny, better known as false albacore, is a member of the mackerel family (*Scombridae*). Most often found in the warm-temperature waters of the Atlantic, this spirited individual ranges as far north as Cape Cod and perhaps New Hampshire in the summer months, with some of the best fishing opportunities in this region found south of Cape Cod along the Rhode Island and Connecticut coasts and south to Chesapeake Bay. The average fish taken weighs between 5 and 8 pounds with some in the double figures possible. It is often found in large schools, near the surface around inlets, bays, and beaches. Here it feeds heavily on squid, fish larvae, herring, and sardines. A wonderful fighter, the false albacore is one of the least-known and under-utilized saltwater species among fly fishermen.

There is a good chance some fly fishermen may have battled this fish and not even realized it, since false albacore are often mistaken for bonito. There are, however, distinguishing markings which separate this fish from others. It has several dark spots—"fishgerprints"—between the pectoral and ventral fins which are not present on related Atlantic species. There are also worm-like marks on the back above the lateral line which never extend forward past the middle of the

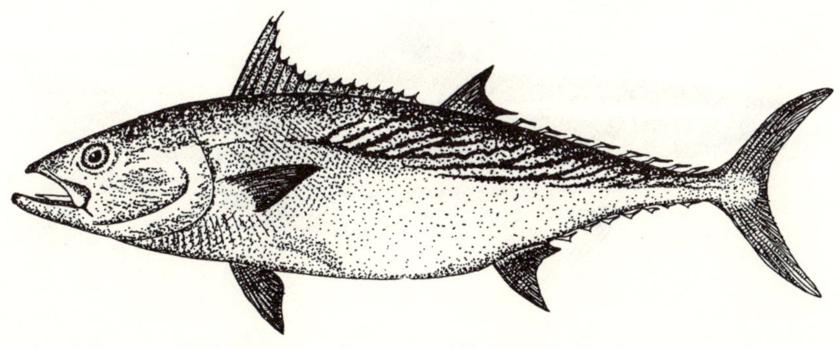

Albacore — *Euthynnus alletteratus*

dorsal fin. This fish has a lower, sloping first dorsal fin. The false albacore has no scales except on the corselet and along the lateral line, and there are no teeth on the vomer.

Because of the possible size of these fish, medium to heavy fishing gear is recommended, anything over 9 feet for a 7, 8, or larger line. The false albacore will accept large bucktails and feathered streamers, and, because they are often found close to the surface, a floating line can be used much of the time.

COBIA *(Rachycentron canadum)*; also Lemon-fish, Black salmon, Black kingfish. The cobia is a predatory fish most frequently found from Cape Cod south, but best known and more abundant further south to Florida and along the Gulf Coast. Although generally more abundant and suited to offshore waters, the cobia is often found well inshore around bays and inlets feeding on crabs, shrimp, and squid. Distinctive in color, this fish is a chocolate-brown shade along the back, the sides lighter, but having alternate stripes of brown and silver running

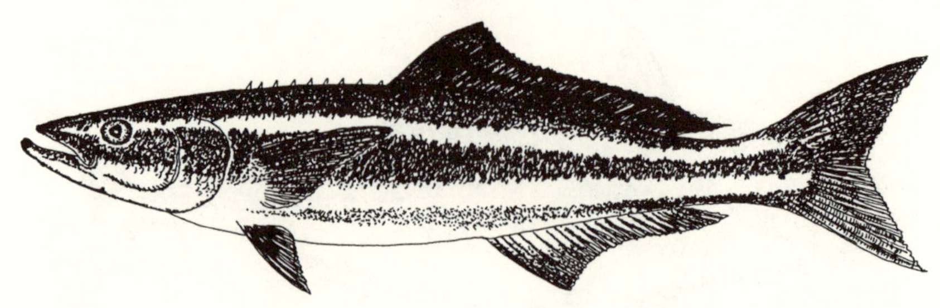

Cobia — *Rachycentron canadum*

along the body. It has a long, broad, depressed head, and a dorsal fin consisting of 8–10 soft spines not connected by a membrane. The second dorsal fin has 1 spine and perhaps 27–33 soft rays.

On medium to heavy fly fishing gear, the cobia is a magnificent adversary. Fish up to 10–15 pounds are possible and, considering their reputation for long, powerful runs up to 70 and 80 yards with occasional leaps, this is probably one of the finest, yet least known or utilized saltwater species along our coast. Once located they will accept flies, with trolling a productive method. The best fishing in New England will be found along the Massachusetts shore, particularly south of Cape Cod, to Connecticut and Rhode Island, and especially further down the coast to New Jersey, Delaware and Maryland.

POLLOCK *(Pollachius virens)*; also Boston bluefish, Green cod. The pollock is well-known along the New England coast and is found in rivers, bays and estuaries from Maine to Rhode Island and Connecticut. Considered the most active member of the cod family (*Gadidae* family), pollock are often seen chasing baitfish to the surface, and because of this, are often found in tidal rivers, in the surf, with some active fly fishing opportunities possible close to the surface. Excellent pollock angling is also found from New York south to Chesapeake Bay when in season, generally May through October.

The pollock is quite distinguishable and differs from other members of the cod family with three specific characteristics: its lower jaw extends past the upper jaw, its tail is forked, and its lateral line is straight, not arching above the pectoral fins. This fish has 3 dorsal fins, and varies in color from olive-green to greenish-brown, with the flanks a lighter yellowish-green or gray. Although this fish can obtain lengths of 3–3½ feet, smaller examples are most common in shallow waters, with weights between 1 and 3 pounds most common for the fly fisherman. Once hooked, pollock can make strong, powerful runs, often leaping out of the water. They are excellent fare on light to medium gear and will readily accept flies under the right conditions. In most cases a floating fly line used with small streamers and bucktails is best; sizes 4–8. However, a sinking-tip line will often be necessary even in shallow bays and coastal rivers.

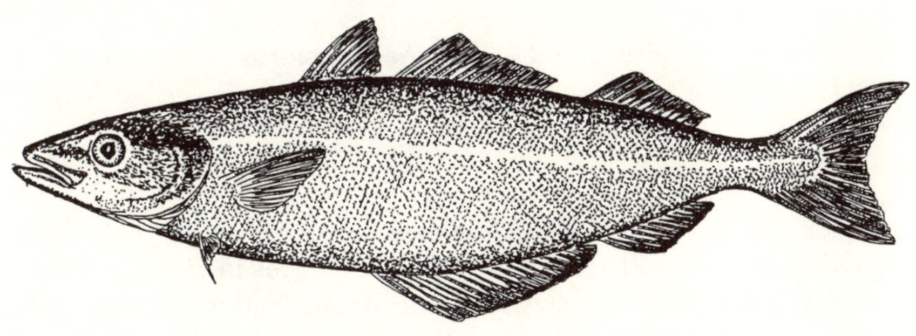

Pollock — *Pollachius virens*

Sand Shark ***(Carcharias taurus).*** This is one of several sharks which are found along the New England and mid-Atlantic coasts. They range from Maine south to Rhode Island and Connecticut in good numbers, and on down to Maryland. Although most commonly found close to the bottom (thus the sub-name Ground shark), they frequent bays, estuaries, and tidal rivers during the summer months, often at fly fishing depths. In most cases, however, the best way to get them in close is by chumming, with flies equipped with Mylar and tied of

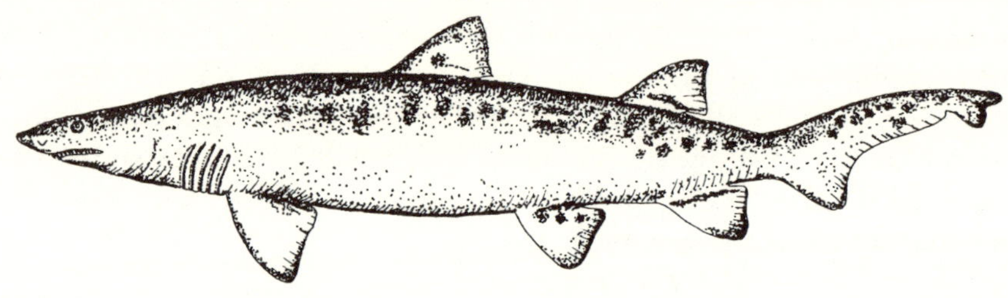

Sand Shark — *Carcharias taurus*

orange or red feathers, and bucktails incorporated with white, being the best lures. You will also need rather large flies in the 2/0–5/0 size and heavy fishing rods, a heavy reel, and strong leader material, in the 30–40 pound test range. These critters grow to lengths of 10½ feet and weigh up to 200 pounds, although 100 pounders are considered big. The average in New England runs 30 to 50 pounds. They hit hard as a rule, are powerful, and are capable of making long, demanding runs. Make sure your reel has plenty of backing.

Sharks are nothing to play around with. Although the sand shark is not generally known as a man-eater, such reports do exist, and they do possess a formidable set of teeth. Once close to the boat, the best way to handle these fish is either to gaff them or simply cut the leader and let them go. Sand sharks have little value for human consumption so there's little sense in keeping them. NEVER put your hands near the mouth, and don't worry about retrieving the fly. There are no bones in sharks, and these fish can wrap themselves around the angler, enabling them to bite, so keep them well away. If you insist on boating them, make sure they are dead first.

WEAKFISH *(Cynoscion regalis)*; also Spotted sea-trout, Squeteague. The weakfish, often called sea-trout, is one of the best known saltwater species along the East Coast, ranging from Cape Cod south to Florida, including the Gulf Coast, with isolated occurrences as far north as Nova Scotia. A few are seen along the coast of Maine and New Hampshire, but the warmer waters to the south are most often preferred. Some of the best weakfish fishing in New England is found off Rhode Island and Connecticut, while mid-Atlantic areas offer excellent opportunities as well.

The weakfish takes the fly well. Popping plugs and streamers of all yellow or red and yellow seem to bring the best results, and flies should be equipped with Mylar strips in the wings. Sizes 2 to 1/0 are best. In some cases, these fish will be found close to the surface, around shallow bays with a grass bottom, where a floating line might do the trick. In most cases, however, you will need a fast-sinking sink-tip or even a lead-core shooting head to get the fly down, since weakfish are often found near the bottom.

The thing to remember about these fish is that they have delicate mouths, hence their name. The hook must be set gently, and the fish must be played gently, too. When hooked, these fish are known to make a long first run, but they are not generally impressive fighters. The real test is to keep the fish on the hook without losing him, which is often difficult due to the tender mouth.

Like other saltwater species, the weakfish can be difficult to find at times, and one of the best ways to "draw" them in is by chumming. Locate an area that looks good, anchor, and start chumming. The fish will often come within yards of the boat, as may several other species worth casting for including mackerel, blues, stripers, and sharks.

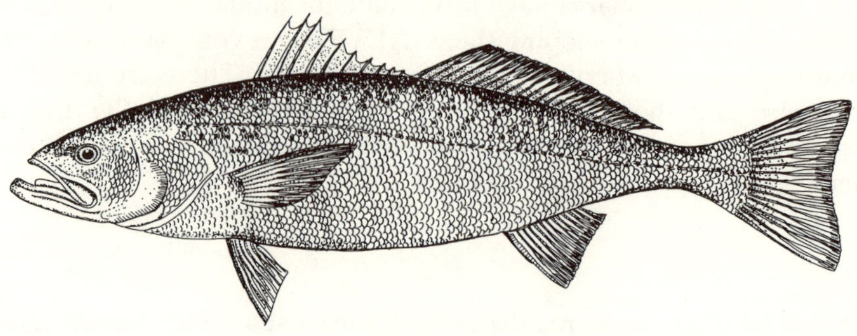

Weakfish — *Cynoscion regalis*

Weakfish grow to good size, with examples up to 10 and 11 pounds possible. The world fly rod record on 4-pound test tippet in 1987 weighed 7 pounds 11 ounces, taken near Fairfield, Connecticut, but the average in waters from Maryland north is between 5 and 6 pounds. You will need light to medium fly gear (8½–9 foot rods) and leaders in the 8–10 pound test class.

SPOTTED SEA TROUT *(Cynoscion nebulosus)*; also Spotted weakfish, Spotted squeteague. Throughout its native range along the northern Atlantic coast, the spotted sea trout has always been one of the most popular and sought after saltwater game species. Populations are found as far north as Cape Cod in Massachusetts but some of the very best fishing from mid-May through October, even perhaps in early December, will be found from New York south along the New Jersey shore to Delaware and particularly Chesapeake Bay. They are most often found inshore in bays, tidal rivers and estuaries during the warm weather months, with some of the larger fish moving offshore during the winter.

In appearance, the sea trout closely resembles the weakfish, a close relative, and it takes a good eye to tell them apart. The body of the sea trout is dark gray above the lateral line, mixing to a sky-blue color below, shading into a silver along the belly. There are numerous round black spots on the field of gray which extend to the tail and onto the dorsal and caudal fins. The first dorsal fin has 10 spines and the second has 1 spine followed by 24 to 26 rays. The anal fin has 2 spines preceded by 10 to 11 soft rays. The body is elongated, like freshwater trout, and the head is relatively small in relation to the rest of the body. All in all, the spotted sea trout is a rather handsome individual.

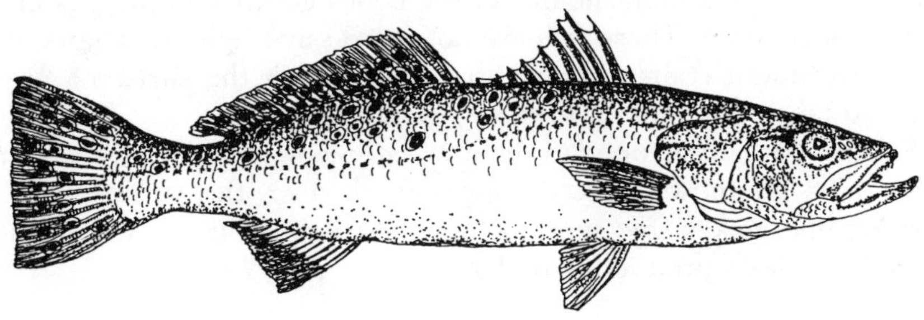

Spotted Sea Trout — *Cynoscion nebulosus*

Along with this they are fun to catch on light to medium fly fishing gears, averaging around 4 pounds and reaching weights up to 8 pounds in this area, and they are excellent eating.

From a fly fishing perspective, sea trout are worthwhile game fish. They reach good size, are available in good numbers for a long period of time, take streamers and bucktails readily and provide a respectable battle once hooked. Streamers of white/black, white/green, white/blue, green, blue, yellow, red/yellow, red and red/white, all with strips of Mylar in the wings are popular in sizes 1/0 to 2. These same colors work well on weakfish, too, in the same sizes.

Keep two things in mind when looking for spotted sea trout. First, these fish are typically bottom feeders and, although at times they can be found at just about any depth, on most occasions it is necessary to go down for them. Fly fishing tactics usually call for sinking lines and allowing time for the line to reach the bottom on each cast before retrieving. Look for them wherever shrimp are available. This is their main food source and when on hand sea trout feed on them exclusively. Other popular foods with sea trout include mullet and menhaden. A keel hook allows the fly fisherman to touch the bottom without getting snagged, and this is where you want to fish.

Second, sea trout (as well as weakfish) have extremely delicate mouths. Fly fishermen should set the hooks gently and play them as lightly as possible. These fish are not impressive fighters when compared to bluefish, for example, but they splash the surface a great deal, so take your time in bringing them in.

Sea trout are often found in shallow water looking for sea worms and other bait. At these times a popper worked on the surface with a floating line makes fine sport, although streamers in the colors suggested are more productive by far.

Dolphin *(Coryphaena hippurus)*; also Dorado. One of the most spectacular fighters available to the fly fisherman is the dolphin, a fish found mostly offshore from Cape Cod south but which also frequents inshore waters where warm currents are found. Dolphin can reach weights in excess of 20 pounds, but the average caught between southern New England and Chesapeake Bay run 5 to 15 pounds. Still, they are powerful individuals capable of stripping off considerable lengths of line. Once hooked, dolphin may skyrocket out of the water and possess amazing power. As a rule, sturdy fly fishing gear is required, something along the lines of a 9–9½ foot rod, size 8 or 9 weight lines, strong leaders and hooks ranging in sizes from 2/0 to 2. Lighter equipment can be used for the smaller school dolphin, but for the bigger ones, the heavier gear is best.

When found offshore, seaweed rips are favorite feeding areas, but they may be found lingering around any floating object. When found

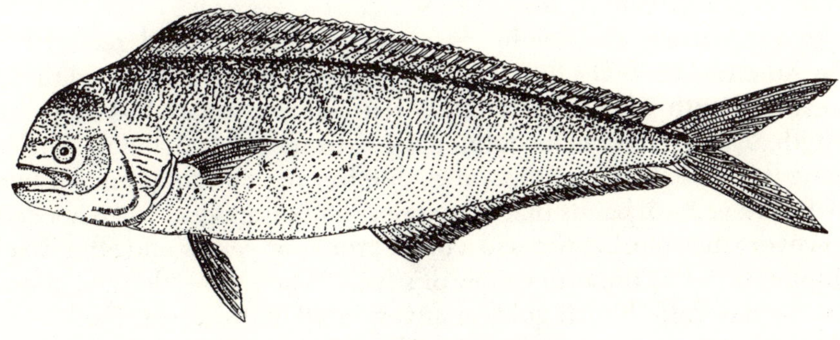

Dolphin — *Coryphaena hippurus*

in these areas, dolphin can be taken by casting with large feather-wing streamers and poppers, providing rather exciting sport. When using poppers, floating lines are sufficient, but with streamers a sinking line is best, and it is generally best to use chum to get the dolphin within casting distance.

At other times, a popular tactic is to troll bait, drawing fish into the slipstream. Once the dolphin takes notice and is in pursuit, reeling in the bait and keeping it dangling in the water next to the boat once it is stopped will keep it close at hand. Generally one baitfish will keep dolphin within easy casting distance but chumming with cut bait may be necessary. This is a good way to take scores of fish when they are found in schools. Remember to look for the seaweed rips and other floating debris, both favorite haunts of the dolphin. Keep in mind, too that dolphin are often found when trolling for other big game such as sailfish. Fishermen looking for some exciting action may wish to keep a fly rod on hand and cast to them when the opportunity arises.

Flies which provide a lot of action in the water regardless of color seem to do well on dolphin. The key here is to provide plenty of action and work the streamer with a fast retrieve. Anything that will draw their attention is apt to work under the right conditions, with the strike typically coming fast.

In appearance, the dolphin is one of the most colorful gamefish in the Atlantic. Its body design signals power, being slender with the greatest depth of the body being four or five times less than the length. The heads of male dolphin are extremely high, almost vertical along the nose. When in the water, dolphin are a bright greenish-blue with dark vertical bands that may appear and disappear. Once hooked, however, the coloring turns to a blue, green, or yellow and after death dolphin turn to a uniform yellow or silver. When alive, dolphin generally display gold, bluish-gold, or silvery-gold on the lower flanks, and silver-white or yellow on the tail. The sides are sprinkled with a mix of dark and light spots ranging from black or blue to a golden color. The dorsal fin is rich blue, and the anal fin is gold or silver. To say the least, they are spectacular to the eye, and a joy to catch.

THE ANADROMOUS SPECIES: ATLANTIC SALMON, COHO SALMON, SEA-RUN BROWN TROUT, AND SHAD

Anadromous fish species are those which migrate from the sea into freshwater rivers and streams to spawn. In all cases, these fish are actually born in freshwater environments and, after spending a specific amount of time there, move into the salt, where they mature into adults. Some of the best known examples are the Atlantic salmon and shad. (The striped bass is also anadromous, but because much of the best angling for them is in the salt, they are rarely thought of as such.)

New England offers several exciting and challenging anadromous fish species. The only Atlantic salmon fishing in the United States is found here, as are some of the country's finest shad rivers. New England also now offers coho salmon, implants from the west, which seem to be doing well; sea-run browns, which have been introduced to a number of coastal rivers in Maine and Massachusetts; and sea-run brook trout, which have been around for decades. The fishing for shad and Atlantic salmon is best in the early spring before many saltwater species arrive, and the fishing for sea-run browns and brookies is best in the fall after the saltwater species have moved south. Further south, shad are found in New York, New Jersey, and Maryland.

Although these fish are not true saltwater inhabitants and much of the best angling for them is in fresh and brackish water (shad, coho salmon, and the trouts are frequently taken in saline conditions, however), we will cover them here simply because the fishing opportunities they offer are too great to overlook.

ATLANTIC SALMON *(Salmo salar).* Atlantic sea-run salmon were once found along the entire New England coast from Maine south to Connecticut and Rhode Island. Each spring they would make annual runs upriver, fighting all obstacles to reach ancestral spawning grounds; some, hundreds of miles from the sea. Within two hundred years after the white man arrived, however, ninety percent of the native runs had been extinguished, with only a handful of rivers in Maine remaining productive.

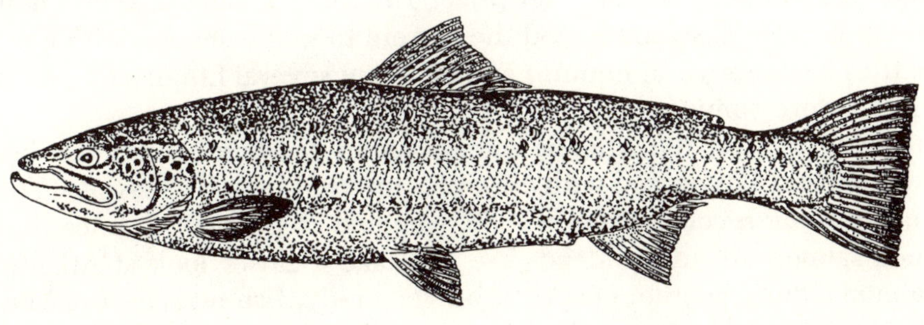

Atlantic Salmon — *Salmo salar*

Today, a gallant effort is being made to bring the Atlantic salmon back to rivers where they once had seemed numberless. Attempts are being made on the Connecticut and Merrimack rivers costing millions of dollars, thus far with limited success. Hopefully, the day will come when the salmon will be found in large numbers, although it is highly unlikely they will ever be as abundant as they once were.

Today, Maine offers the only fishing for Atlantic salmon in the United States. All fishing is by fly fishing only and many regulations and specific bag limits apply; a special license is required. All interested fishermen should carefully check the current "Atlantic Sea-Run Salmon Fishing Regulations," available from the Maine Atlantic Sea-Run Salmon Commission, P.O. Box 1298, Bangor, Maine 04401, or the Maine Department of Inland Fisheries and Wildlife, 284 State St., Augusta, Maine 04333.

To say Atlantic salmon fishing is "exciting" would not be doing it justice somehow. It is, in my opinion, one of the angling world's great sports, with the Atlantic salmon itself the best fighting fish in fresh water. To catch one of these individuals takes patience, knowledge of the fish itself, skill with a fly rod, and luck in being in the right place at the right time. Once the fish is hooked, the story has only just begun. The salmon has the ability to strip out 100 yards of line and backing with ease in powerful, leaping runs which have made him a famous and highly sought-after prize. The Atlantic salmon knows how to use its power, strength, and the current to its advantage, with most battles lasting several minutes and covering several hundred yards of river before coming to an end.

In most cases, the Atlantic salmon found in Maine rivers run between 6 and 12 pounds, with examples up to 17 pounds possible. The current state record, taken in 1980, weighed 28 pounds, 1 ounce, but such salmon are rare indeed. We will take a closer look at Atlantic salmon fishing in other chapters, but generally, fishing is best in May and June in such rivers as the Penobscot, Dennys, St. Croix, Machias, Narraguagus, Sheepscot, and East Machias on flies such as the Cosseboom, Black Bear Hair flies, Coburn Special and Durham Ranger.

COHO SALMON *(Oncorhynchus kisutch).* Coho salmon are not native to the East Coast, but since the late 1960's they have been available in a few rivers in Massachusetts and New Hampshire. Massachusetts introduced the species to its North River system in 1969, with New Hampshire following shortly thereafter with introductions to its Lamprey River, near Newmarket. Both fisheries have experienced ups and downs over the years, but there is no doubt that there is growing interest in the coho among New England anglers, and that the coho provides an interesting and exciting challenge for those who take the time to seek him out.

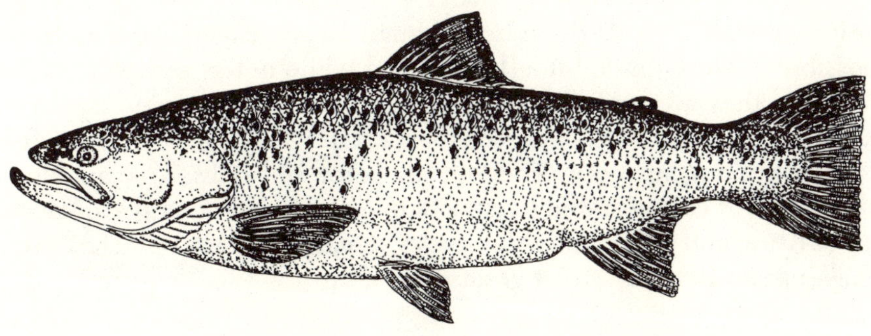

Coho Salmon — *Oncorhynchus kisutch*

The coho salmon is native to the Pacific Coast, particularly northern California, the Pacific Northwest, the west coast of Canada, and Alaska; unlike Atlantic salmon, they die after spawning. When found in salt water and for a short time after entering fresh water, they are bright silver in color, having black spots on the back, upper sides, base of dorsal fin, and upper lobe of the tail. Upon entering fresh water, however, the males experience a dramatic color change, turning crimson and developing a "kype", with both the upper and lower jaw becoming extended and hooked toward each other, making it impossible for them to close their mouths. The females, on the other hand, change very little, with the only obvious change being that they turn a little darker with a reddish or pinkish stripe or tint along the sides. Both sexes during the spawning stage are magnificent specimens, and are powerhouses on the end of a rod.

The best fishing for coho salmon occurs in the fall, generally from September through late November. They are taken on lures when found in bays, with both lures and flies good once entering fresh water. Fishermen will require a stout fly rod, a medium reel with sufficient backing, and flies in the 2 to 2/0 sizes. More specific information on how and where to fly fish for coho salmon and which flies to use is provided in Chapters 3, 5, and 6.

These fish weigh anywhere from 4 to 11 pounds, with the average being around 7 to 10 pounds, although larger examples are always possible. Coho salmon hit a fly hard and while not as aerobatic as the Atlantic, they are quite impressive, having the stamina and power to make fairly long runs. I think the most exciting aspect about these fish is their bulldog strength. They hit like a ton of bricks, are capable of stripping out considerable lengths of line and backing, and are known for twisting and rolling into the leader, trying to break off. They are a challenge to fish for, and a great deal of fun.

SEA-RUN BROWN TROUT ***(Salmo trutta).*** Sea-run brown trout have been known to fishermen in Europe for generations but anglers in New England have been familiar with them only since the late 1950's. At that time, Connecticut experimented with a European strain of sea-trout in a few of its coastal streams, establishing a moderate fishery for huge fish. Unfortunately, angler interest was not high, and for all practical purposes, the fishery no longer exists.

In the early 1970's, however, Massachusetts took up the cause, and now provides some exciting and productive opportunities in seven coastal rivers, mostly on or near Cape Cod. These rivers and streams are: Scorton Creek, the Mashpee, Childs, Quashnet, Marston Mills, Santuit (Cotuit), and Coonamessett rivers.

In 1976, after witnessing the success in Massachusetts, Maine started its own sea-run trout fishery. Three southern coastal streams

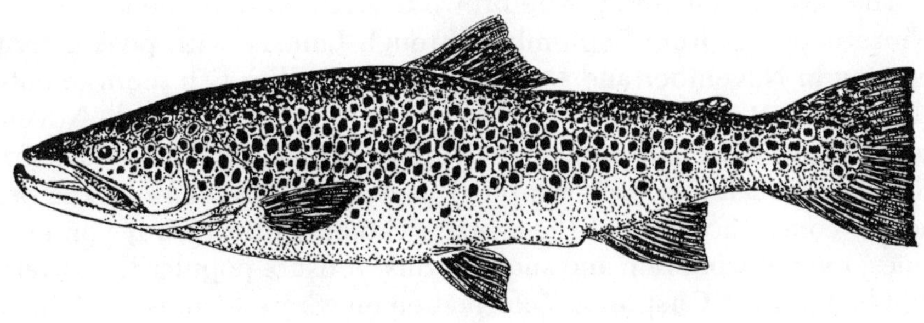

Sea-Run Brown Trout — *Salmo trutta*

were originally selected for study and annual stocking, but at present (1989) only two rivers, the Ogunquit in York County and the Royal River in Cumberland County, offer sea-run populations. Both fisheries are doing well and there are future plans to expand the program. In all cases, in Massachusetts and Maine, fishing interest and pressure is not high considering the number of anglers in each state, but among those who have taken the time to experience casting a fly for sea-run browns, there is a deep interest and avid following.

Because of the abundant food supply available to these fish, growth rate is high, with fish up to 6 and 9 pounds being reported in some Massachusetts waters. In Maine the fish run smaller as a rule (between 2 and 4 pounds), although the Royal, which is known for producing larger but fewer fish than the Ogunquit, has produced fish up to 6 pounds in years past. In most cases, these trout are fat, robust individuals with a fighting spirit much more powerful than freshwater counterparts. They accept a fly voraciously and are capable of making long runs, hating to come to the net.

The fly fisherman will require a rod of at least 8½ feet, with a 9-footer best, designed for a 6, 7, or 8 weight line. Leaders in the 4–8 pound test class are advised. A list of productive flies is included in Chapter 3.

The best fishing for sea-run brown trout in both Maine and Massachusetts occurs from September through January with peak activity coming in November and December. The smaller fish seem to enter the river first, generally in mid-to-late September and early November, followed by the larger specimens, which remain in the area through the fall and early winter. I have found that some of the best action comes in some of the worst weather under cloudy, ominous skies, even during rain and snow storms. A list of popular fly patterns will be found in Chapter 3. Information on where to go is available in Chapter 6.

SHAD *(Alosa sapidissima).* The American shad, like the Atlantic salmon, once constituted a prosperous commercial fishery along the New England coast. When our ancestors first arrived here, shad were even more numerous than salmon, with over twenty rivers in Maine alone supporting commercial fisheries of some degree. Traditionally, the largest runs were found on the Androscoggin, Kennebec, Penobscot, and St. Croix rivers in Maine, the Merrimack in Massachusetts and New Hampshire, and the Connecticut, which travels into the heart of New England as far as Vermont and northern New Hampshire. Like the Atlantic salmon, many native runs have declined substantially, although a number of rivers, including the Connecticut, Merrimack, Penobscot, Narraguagus, Kennebec, and Androscoggin still provide good runs which support a sports fishery. Smaller fisheries are found in a number of other rivers along the coast, from Maine to Connecticut and Rhode Island, and attempts are being made to reintroduce the shad to a number of ancestral rivers such as the Pawcatuck and Hunt rivers in Rhode Island.

The shad is silver in color, possessing a single dorsal fin in the middle of the back. There is a large spot, usually black, directly behind the top of the gill cover, which is followed by several more spots which are smaller than the first. The tail of the fish is deeply forked, and the lower jaw is entirely enclosed within the upper when the two are pressed together. Shad have large, rather loose scales, and may weigh up to 12 pounds. The average fish taken by the fly fisher-

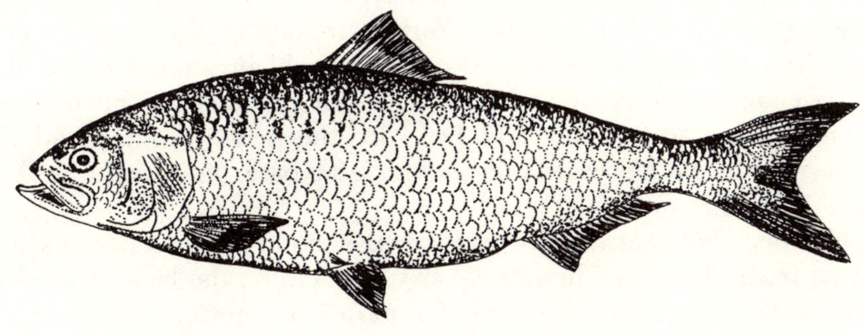

Shad — *Alosa sapidissima*

man runs 2 to 8 pounds. They are strong, powerful individuals, particularly when found in moving water; they often leap once hooked. They are exciting adversaries on light to medium weight fly gear, and fly fishing is often considered one of the finest ways to catch them. Next to the Atlantic salmon, shad are my favorite anadromous species, and I usually make three or four trips each spring to New England hotspots to try my luck.

More detailed information on how to fly fish for shad, which flies to use, and more information on tackle will be provided later in this text (Chapters 3, 5, and 6). Generally, however, nearly all fishing is done below the surface with weighted wet flies. You will need a high-density sinking line and a stout rod. On some New England rivers wading is possible, and when you find shad in a shallow stretch, this is the ultimate way to go. In other areas, a small boat or canoe is needed. The best fishing is found in the spring, particularly in late April, through May into early June. The time of peak runs differs according to locality, water, and weather conditions, but generally, the angler will find shad available during this period.

South of New England, American shad are found in several rivers, down to Chesapeake Bay. In New York they make spring runs into the

Hudson, in the Delaware between New Jersey and Pennsylvania, moving well upstream into New York State, and in Maryland American shad will also be found and can be caught in such rivers as the Susquehanna, Patuxent and Potomac—all the way to the nation's capital. Here again, May and June are the prime months and fly fishermen in these areas would use the same basic equipment used in New England.

Hickory shad (*Alosa mediocris*) are also found in many of the same rivers from Maine to Chesapeake Bay. Generally, the hickory shad is smaller than the American shad with most fish running 1 to 3 pounds with a maximum around 6 pounds. Among anglers, the hickory shad is not as popular, although it is a lot of fun on light fly gear. The two shads are easily identified—the jaw of the hickory version is long and extends beyond the nose or upper mouth whereas the lower jaw of the American shad is entirely enclosed within the upper jaw when pressed together. Some prime fishing rivers include the Susquehanna and its feeder streams and the Potomac, both in Maryland.

Chapter 3

FLIES, RODS, REELS, AND FLY LINES

Back in the days when saltwater fly fishing was in its infancy, hardly any equipment existed for specific use in a saline environment. The early explorers knew that most game fish being caught on conventional tackle could be taken on a fly—but most of the fly fishing gear available then was intended for freshwater use.

Today, however, all that has changed. The interest in saltwater fly fishing has grown so rapidly that fly patterns specifically designed for anything from bluefish to bonito are now available, as is equipment designed to handle the big saltwater fish and the conditions for both inshore and offshore fly fishing. The sport is continuing to grow so fast that new fly patterns are being introduced all the time, and new products are becoming available almost as fast as those for freshwater use.

I think that selecting your first saltwater fly rod, reel, and line is easier if you keep certain things in perspective. For example, saltwater fly fishing conditions are often more demanding than when fishing a remote pond or trout stream, and the fish are generally bigger, heavier, and more powerful, which means you'll need a rod that is sturdy, one that has some backbone and can throw a line and fly under windy conditions. Today's fly fishermen will find rods specifically designed for saltwater use, although if you have a rod designed for a

6, 7, or 8 weight line and a reel that can handle 150–250 yards of 20-pound test backing, you already have what is needed to get started.

The same is true with fly lines. Great advances have been made in this area in the last twenty years, and, though some lines with a specific taper are better for saltwater use than others, any line will get you by. More on that later.

Perhaps the biggest investment you will have to make when getting started in saltwater fly fishing is in flies. Years ago most fly fishermen seeking mackerel, bonito, bluefish and striped bass used many of the flies we use to catch salmon, trout, and bass today simply because nothing else was available. That, too, has changed, and you will now find dozens of patterns illustrated in books, magazines, and tying guides which you can tie on your own, or which are available at most fly shops. Selecting which patterns to go with is not as complicated in saltwater fishing, since you don't have to worry about dry flies or about imitating the natural, and there are not as many saltwater flies as there are freshwater flies. When going after the anadromous species along the New England and mid-Atlantic coasts, you will find only a half dozen patterns necessary.

This chapter is intended to clear up some of the misconceptions about saltwater fly fishing gear, and to help make the selection of rods, reels, lines, and flies a little easier on the novice. We also hope to illustrate which gear is best and why, to take away some of the fear often associated with saltwater fly fishing.

FLIES

The fly is the meat and potatoes of any fly fishing outfit. Without it there is no chance whatsoever of catching fish, and this is as true in saltwater as it is in fresh.

Compared to most freshwater counterparts, saltwater offerings are rather basic in design—the theory being that saltwater fish are always in a feeding frenzy and are less selective than trout and salmon, for example, so flies do not have to be as imitative or as fancy as those we might use in inland fresh water. I would agree with this to a point and

These epoxy flies, shaped like a shrimp, can be deadly on bottom-feeding species and very productive in shallow water. (Raychard photo)

have caught bluefish, mackerel, and striped bass on some pretty crude contraptions, but I will make a stand when it comes to size, color, buoyancy, and sink rate of a saltwater fly. These are all key factors which govern whether a fly will work consistently and should be considered carefully when tying or buying your selection.

One thing to our advantage when fishing the salt is the fact that insect life as we have come to know and recognize it on freshwater ponds, rivers, and streams is virtually absent. There are no mayflies and caddis, so dry flies are of no importance except when fishing for Atlantic salmon. Since all fish in the sea feed on other fish and crustaceans such as shrimp and crabs, as well as sea worms and sand eels, nearly all of our fishing is done below the surface with streamers and bucktails. (There are exceptions, of course, such as when bluefish are found chopping the surface—but this calls for popping plugs, not dry flies.)

I have come to the conclusion that color or color combinations have a great deal to do with whether a fly will consistently work. Just about all baitfish the larger predators seek out day after day have some blue, green, blue-green, purple, black, brown, or white tint to them. When I started tying flies with these colors, my success ratio increased, and that's why one of my favorite patterns is the Lefty's Deceiver which can be tied with any of these shades and in various combinations. When combined with a few strands of Flashabou, and when tied on the right size hook for the fish you are after, the Deceiver patterns are among the best available for fly fishing off the New England coast. You should always include some white. Exact imitation is not necessary, but I have no doubt that if you construct flies that reasonably imitate local and dominant baitfish you will find more fish on the end of the line.

There are many times when an overly bright or flashy fly is better. They seem to work very well in brackish water conditions and under low light conditions. Flies with purple, red, and orange, generally in conjunction with white, have always been good, as have many of the fluorescent colors, and it is recommended that a few flies with these colors be on hand at all times.

Hook size is important, too. I used to think the bigger the hook the better for saltwater fish, but this is not necessarily true. While bluefish and striped bass generally call for large hooks, bonito rarely accept a fly longer than 3½–4 inches in length, and smaller is most often best. The same is true with mackerel. Flies in sizes from long shanked trolling hooks (4X-Long to 6) seem to produce more mackerel action for me than anything else. While most of your flies will range from size 4/0 and 2/0 down to 1, 2, and 4, and though you should have some flies in each of these sizes, it helps to know which size hook is best for the species of fish you are seeking. This often takes time and trial and error to learn. But by doing so, you can greatly reduce the number of flies in your arsenal, saving time and money, and your success ratio will increase.

The following list will give you a basic idea of what size flies should be used for various species:

Albacore	**2/0–2**
Atlantic salmon	**2–10**
Bluefish	**2/0–2**
Bonito	**1,2,4**
Cobia	**2/0,4/0–2**
Coho salmon	**2,4,6,8**
Dolphin	**2/0–2**
Kingfish	**2/0–2**
Mackerel	**2,4,6**
Pollock	**2,4,6**
Sand shark	**2/0–2**
Sea-run brown trout	**4,6,8**
Sea trout	**1/0–4**
Shad	**4,6,8**
Striped bass	**2/0–2**
Weakfish	**2/0–2,4**

The size of your hook and fly also effects sink rate and silhouette, which are two other characteristics determining whether a fly works the way it should. In many cases a fly must sink to the proper depth before the retrieve, and be at or near the same level as your quarry to entice action, and the way a fly is constructed can help things along. Water conditions, which can vary from clear to murky, dictate how well a fish can see the fly and, therefore, while a sparsely tied fly might be just what you need in a clean bay or open ocean, a more densely tied fly might be necessary in areas where visibility is restricted. This is also true when fishing at night for striped bass, since a bulky fly provides more vibration and is thus easier to locate.

Sink rate can be controlled several ways. Hooks with short shanks and those with a sparse wing sink faster than long-shanked, densely tied counterparts. If you plan on fishing deep it is often best to go with a short-shanked hook with a wing only thick enough to provide the necessary action. When fishing shallow or just below the surface, longer hooks and heavier wings should be used.

Another way to control the sink rate is to incorporate some lead or beads in the fly, although they take a little getting used to when casting. If you insist on a sparse wing when fishing the shallows, a fly

Clockwise, from left: A fly tied tandem-style; fly with a collar around the head to slow its sink rate; standard bucktail; (bottom and center) flies incorporating Flashabou in tail and wing, respectively. (Diane Dery photo)

with a thick collar helps slow the sink rate, too. Finally, you can influence how far down a fly will travel, and how fast, with your fly line and leader. Floating lines and long leaders will help keep a fly on top or close to it, while sinking lines and sink-tips with various densities and shorter leaders will get the offering down.

Another type of fly casting lure that is increasing in popularity, and one which is a lot of fun to use, is the popping plug. This works well when bluefish and striped bass are found in shallow water, or chomping baitfish on the surface. It can even be used to draw fish up from the bottom and is basically intended to impersonate a fish that is in trouble and struggling on the surface. It is made of hair, cork, and plastic, often incorporated with feathers.

The only problem when using popping plugs is that novice anglers often make too much noise with them, either when casting and laying them on the water, or when working them on the surface. Casting these lures properly takes practice, as does giving them the right amount of action, and a poor presentation or excessive motion with a plug can easily spook fish. The best way to use it in most cases is to drop it well away from the target, either to one side or in a spot where the fish will cruise into it, and work it to him, giving it only enough action to arouse interest, imitating a fish in trouble. Popping plugs come in various sizes and colors, and you should have a good selection on hand.

It should be noted that saltwater flies can be tied on either stainless steel or carbon steel hooks. Proponents of carbon steel hooks insist they are stronger and will dissolve in salt water in case of break-off. The unfortunate thing about carbon steel hooks is that they will rust. Stainless steel, on the other hand, will not rust. I find them to be strong enough to hold even the largest fish off the New England coast and have never had one bend under pressure. Most commercially available saltwater flies are tied on stainless, largely due to their non-rusting characteristic. Both are good, and which you use is more of a personal choice than anything else.

In either case, make sure your saltwater flies are sharp, especially the larger hook sizes, since sizes larger than 2 which are made of bigger gauge wire and have good-sized barbs are difficult to drive home. You want a hook that will penetrate on the strike and, because many saltwater species have tough, bony mouths, a sharp point and cutting edge is necessary.

It is highly recommended that you have a file on hand at all times and make sure your hooks are touched up before going to work. It is also a good idea to check them periodically after catching fish, sharpening when necessary. If you tie your own, it is much easier to put a point and cutting edge on while the hook is in the vise before tying the fly. To keep the file from rusting while fishing, simply spray it with gun oil or WD-40® and keep it in a small plastic sheath or bag.

The following list provides some productive and popular saltwater and anadromous fly patterns:

POPULAR SALTWATER FLIES

KEY: STRIPED BASS-SB, BLUEFISH-BF, BONITO-B, MACKEREL-M, ALBACORE-AL, COBIA-CO, POLLOCK-PK, SHARK-SH, WEAKFISH-WF, KINGFISH-KF, DOLPHIN-DLP, SEA TROUT-ST

Lefty's Deceiver (in various color combinations)	**SB,M,WF**
Seaducer	**SB,B,WF**
Platinum Blonde (also, Honey Blonde, Argentine Blonde, and Strawberry Blonde)	**SB,M,B,KF,ST**
Apple Blossom Marabou	**SB**
Blackberry Blossom Marabou	**SB**
Horror	**B**
Blockbuster	**SB,BF,CO**
Palmer Diller	**SB,BF,B,AL**
Gibbs Striper Fly	**BF,SB,B,AL,CO,KF,DLP,ST**
Loving Bass Fly	**BF,SB,B,AL,CO,KF,ST**
Sands Bonefish	**B,WF**
Buds Sand Eel	**SB,BF,B,PK,ST**
Hamanda Silversides	**SB,BF,B,WF,PK,ST,KF**
Glass Minnow (white and green versions)	**B,BF,M,WF**
Black Sheep (black/red, green/yellow, blue/white versions)	**B,SB,WF,CO**
Ka-Boom Popper	**SB,B,BF**
Bud's Eel	**SB,BF,B,WF,PK,ST**
Armand's Striper Tracker	**SB,BF**
Dan's Offshore	**SB,B,WF,PK**
Janssen Halfbeak	**SH,BF,SB**
Herb Chase Striper Fly	**SB,B,PK,WF,M,KF,DLP**
Herring Fly	**M,B,WF,CO,KF,ST**
Janssen Striper Fly	**SB,B,PK,WF**
Yellow Skipping Bug	**SB,B,BF,DLP**

FLIES FOR THE ANADROMOUS SPECIES

ATLANTIC SALMON
- Cosseboom
- Black Bear Green Butt
- Durham Ranger
- Rusty Rat
- Silver Rat
- Blue Charm
- Muddler
- Black Dose
- Green Highlander

ATLANTIC SALMON/DRY FLIES
- Royal Wulff
- Grey Wulff
- MacIntosh
- Pink Lady
- Brown Bivisible
- Badger Bivisible
- Bomber
- Mickey Finn

COHO SALMON
- Cardinelle
- Colonel Bates
- Mickey Finn
- Orange Matuka
- Orange Marabou
- Platinum Blonde
- Strawberry Blonde

(Many of the bright Atlantic salmon flies work on coho salmon, too.)

SEA-RUN BROWN TROUT
- Finger Mullet
- Sand Eel
- Janssen Shrimp Fly
- Herring Fly
- Jewette's Blue Crab
- Polar Shrimp
- Sand Flea
- Shrimp Fly
- Black Matuka
- Olive Matuka
- Black Zonker
- Olive Zonker
- Matuka Sculpin
- Muddler

SHAD
- Shad Bump
- Nat's Favorite
- Chesapeake Bay Shad Fly
- Red Marabou

RODS

Fly fishing in salt water is considerably different from that done in fresh water. We are searching for bigger fish, as a rule, heavier fish, casting bigger and heavier flies, and, very often, under difficult wind conditions. When fighting fish down deep we must lift them off the bottom, which we rarely do with salmon and trout.

To tackle these and other situations, we need a rod with some backbone, yet something we can handle when casting. Freshwater rods under 8½ feet in length don't have the muscle for most saltwater action, nor are they recommended for Atlantic salmon, coho salmon, shad, and other anadromous species. A longer rod of stiff action is best, especially those designed for 7, 8, and 9 weight lines.

It should be understood, however, that there is no one rod capable of handling every situation in the salt. Where you might get away with using an 8½ foot rod for mackerel and sea-run browns, you will never make it with a rod of this length on big bluefish, striped bass, bonito, and Atlantic salmon unless you happen to be an exceptional caster and have experience fighting powerful fish. Along the New England and mid-Atlantic coasts and in our coastal rivers, a rod of 9–9½ feet is perhaps the best way to go. These rods are long enough to help lift the line and fly off or out of the water, possess great casting capabilities under all conditions, and make changing directions when casting easier—yet are short enough to handle rather easily and have the power to control and lift big fish.

Of course, the type of action you prefer in a fly rod is a personal thing. When using dry flies on a trout stream, a soft, slow-action rod, one that bends well down into the mid-section is best for soft delivery. But when working for the bigger and more powerful saltwater and anadromous species, a stiffer, fast-action rod is often best simply because it has better lifting power which you will sometimes need. I also think once you get used to a fast-action stick you will find that it is better designed to handle a wider array of hook sizes and fishing conditions.

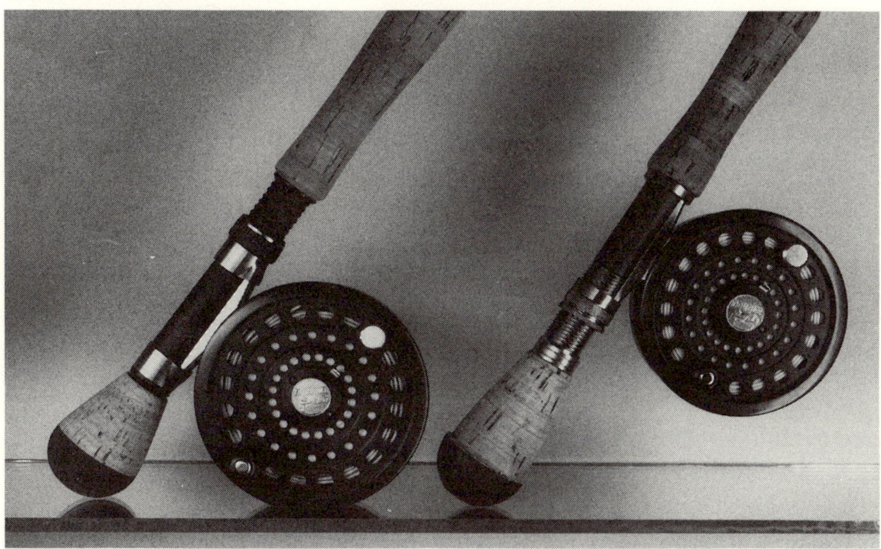

Rods with extension butts provide greater leverage and control. Extension butts with rubber tips are best. (Raychard/Gorham photo)

One thing your saltwater rod should have is an extension butt, a short 2-or-3-inch addition that either slides into the handle or is a permanent part of the rod that can be screwed out whenever you want it. Some fishermen don't like extension butts since fly lines can snag on them while casting or when shooting, but I think their advantages outweigh this slight disadvantage. They provide extra leverage on bigger fish, offer a pivot point when you have to pump the rod, and help keep the reel away from your body when winding in line.

Modern fly rods are made of several different materials: bamboo, fiberglass, graphite, and boron; and the type we buy is often determined by how much we want to spend. For saltwater fishing, bamboo rods are the least practical. They are expensive and have limitations which should be respected.

Fiberglass fly rods are still the backbone of saltwater angling. They are less expensive than graphite and boron counterparts, although they are heavier, and are extremely rugged. Fiberglass was the first synthetic material used to make fly rods back in the 1940's, and they have steadily improved since then. The material does have its limitations, however. Fiberglass is lighter than bamboo and must have a greater bend to deliver the same amount of power. Also, fiberglass rods are quicker to reach their load limits on long, powerful casts, and will "break down" faster than graphite, boron, or graphite/boron rods. Fiberglass rods are also more difficult to work with and are less forgiving of casting mistakes. These limitations, however, are seldom a problem, and the fiberglass fly rod continues to be very popular. It is highly recommended for the novice or experienced angler.

Graphite and boron/graphite rods are excellent saltwater tools and have probably saved the day for many enthusiasts due to their lightness and strength. Although more expensive than fiberglass rods, if you plan to continue your saltwater fishing and want to purchase a rod that can handle almost any situation and throw flies and poppers with relative ease, graphite or boron is the way to go. These rods possess several qualities which I like. They are very light and easy to work with for long periods of time. (A 9-foot bamboo rod, for example, may weigh 7 or 8 ounces, a fiberglass perhaps in the neighborhood of 6 ounces, but a graphite or boron of that length will weigh only 3 ounces!) A couple of ounces may not seem like a lot, but when making hundreds of casts in a day's outing, it can save considerable strain on your casting arm. These rods are also very strong and have a high degree of elasticity, meaning that they resist bending, which makes them stiffer. Because of this, the fly fisherman is able to get a longer length of line into the air with less bend in the rod, there is less time between the forward and back cast, and the loops on the back cast are smaller, cutting down on resistance—all of which increases line speed and line momentum, allowing the line to travel greater distances with less effort. Graphite and boron rods are also more forgiving about casting mistakes. And, because these rods are stiffer than fiberglass rods, they possess greater lifting power, which is sometimes needed in moving big fish off the bottom.

The following chart lists some recommended fly rods for saltwater fishing from New England south to Chesapeake Bay:

MAKER/MATERIAL	MODEL	LENGTH	ROD WEIGHT	LINE WEIGHT
Berkley/graphite	Lightning	8½ ft.	N/A	7–8
Berkley/graphite	Phazer	8½ ft.	N/A	7–8
Berkley/graphite	Grayfite	8½ ft.	N/A	8
Berkley/fiberglass	Avenger	8 ft.**	N/A	7
Cortland/graphite	Black Diamond	8½–9 ft.	2¾–4½ oz.	6,7,8,9,10
Cortland/graphite	Leon Chandler Signature Rods	8½–9 ft.	2¾–3½ oz.	6,7,8
Cortland/graphite	LTD Series	8½–9 ft.	3⅛–3½ oz.	6,7,8
Cabela's/graphite	Fish Eagle II	8½–9½ ft.	N/A	6–12
Cabela's/graphite	Traditional Fish Eagle	8½–9½ ft.	N/A	6,7,8,9
Daiwa/graphite	KGX Series	8½–9 ft.	N/A	8
Daiwa/graphite	Apollo Gold Series	8½–9 ft.	N/A	7,8
Daiwa/graphite	1000 Series	8 ft.**	N/A	7
Fenwick/graphite	HMG Series	8½–9½ ft.	3½–4¾ oz.	6,7,8,9,10
Fenwick/graphite	Eagle Graphite Series	8½–9 ft.	3⅛–3⅜ oz.	6,8
Fenwick/boron	Boron-X Series	8½–9½ ft.	3⅞–5½ oz.	6,7,8,9,10
Fenwick/fiberglass	Fenwick Fiberglass	8½–9 ft.	3⅜–4½ oz.	6,7,8,9,10

**Certain rods of 8 feet can be used on saltwater and anadromous fish species, especially those made of graphite and boron, since they have a stiff action (if you plan to have more than one rod in your arsenal). If you plan on going with one rod for the time being and want to fish for all species under varied conditions, a 9–9½ foot rod is recommended.

MAKER/MATERIAL	MODEL	LENGTH	ROD WEIGHT	LINE WEIGHT
L.L. Bean/graphite	Atlantic Salmon	9 ft.	$3\frac{7}{8}$ oz.	8
L.L. Bean/graphite	Light Tarpon	9 ft.	$4\frac{1}{4}$ oz.	10
L.L. Bean/graphite	Big Salmon	$9\frac{1}{2}$ ft.	$4\frac{1}{2}$ oz.	10
L.L. Bean/graphite	Trophy Tarpon	9 ft.	$5\frac{1}{2}$ oz.	12
Orvis/graphite	Advantage Series	9 ft., 3 in.	$4\frac{1}{4}$ oz.	7
Orvis/graphite	Powerhouse	$8\frac{1}{2}$ ft.	$2\frac{7}{8}$ oz.	8
Orvis/graphite	Rivermaster	$9\frac{1}{2}$ ft.	$3\frac{5}{8}$ oz.	8
Orvis/graphite	Light Salmon/Saltwater	$9\frac{1}{2}$ ft.	$4\frac{1}{8}$ oz.	8
Orvis/graphite	Shooting Star	9 ft.	$4\frac{1}{4}$ oz.	9
Orvis/fiberglass	Full-Flex A Series	$8\frac{1}{2}$ ft.	$3\frac{1}{2}$ oz.	8
Sage/graphite	Sage RPL	9 ft.	$3\frac{1}{8}$ oz.	7
Sage/graphite	Sage RPL	9 ft.	$3\frac{1}{2}$ oz.	8
Sage/graphite	Sage RPL X Saltwater	9 ft.	4 oz.	9
Sage/graphite	Sage RPL X Saltwater	9 ft.	4 oz.	10
Sage/graphite	Sage RPL X Saltwater	9 ft.	6 oz.	11
Sage/graphite	Sage RPL X Saltwater	9 ft.	6 oz.	12
Sage/graphite	Sage RPL X Saltwater	9 ft.	N/A	13
St. Croix/graphite	Imperial XL Series	$8\frac{1}{2}$–10 ft.	$3\frac{1}{4}$–6 oz.	6/7,7/8,8/9,9/10
St. Croix/graphite	Pro Graphite Series	$8\frac{1}{2}$–9 ft.	$3\frac{1}{4}$–$4\frac{1}{2}$ oz.	6/7,8/9

REELS

I have always thought that the fly reel is one of the most important tools for the saltwater fly fisherman. In many freshwater situations, we play the fish from the line, but most saltwater fish are played directly from the reel, which means reels should be slightly bigger and stronger than those we use on trout. The typical freshwater reel may weigh between 3 and 6 ounces, while saltwater counterparts weigh anywhere from 6 to 12 ounces. Saltwater reels are also more costly (with some models ten times that of a freshwater reel) but, if you plan on doing a great deal of saltwater fishing, there is no doubt they are well worth the investment in the long run.

This does not mean to say the fly fisherman should immediately invest several hundred dollars in a Billy Pate reel. I have caught hundreds of mackerel, bluefish, and striped bass on my Pfleuger Medalists and Valentine reels, and have experienced little trouble. For their size and price they will suffice; chances are, the reel you already have will get you by, providing it is capable of taking at least 200 yards of backing.

There are basically three different types of fly reels: automatic reels, single action reels, and multiplying reels. Of these, the automatic type is the least useful for salt water since its drag system is poor, it carries too little line, and its mechanical parts corrode easily and quickly. There is also some problem in finding and switching spools on automatic reels. Multiplying reels are a little better. These reels pick up line faster due to their gear system, but the gears and the design of these reels sacrifice strength and durability. Salt water also gets into the moving parts, which causes problems.

Automatic and multiplying reels can be quite useful when fishing for Atlantic salmon, shad, and coho salmon in freshwater environments. Atlantic salmon, for example, often make fast runs towards the fisherman, at which times these reels help pick up excess line in a hurry.

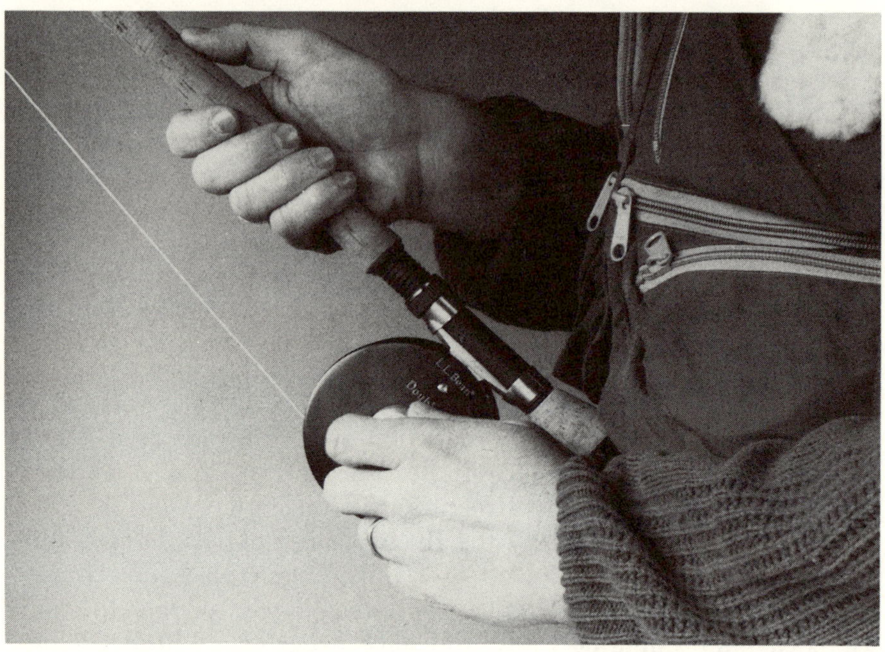

The drag adjustment screw should be large enough to locate easily, and the adjustment range should be large. (Raychard/Gorham photo)

If you want to settle on one type of reel, however, it is best to go with a single action which can be used anywhere. Most fly fishermen with saltwater experience prefer a single action reel, and most of the top reels are based on its simple yet dependable design. Because there are fewer moving parts, single action reels are more trouble-free, and most of the better brands are much stronger and more reliable than automatic or multiplying reels.

Most saltwater fly reels are nothing more than upscaled versions of freshwater reels that we use for trout, bass, and landlocked salmon. The reason they are bigger and more expensive is that they are designed to handle more backing and line and are made of a solid bar of aluminum, most often turned on a lathe and entirely handcrafted. The reels are then anodized to prevent corrosion, and, because of their precision, craftsmanship, and materials, will last a lifetime. Some saltwater reels are made of brass, which is resistant to corrosive saltwater. Although most of the reels are basically the same in concept, designs do vary from make to make and which you choose is up to you.

There are certain things you should check for when making a purchase. Make sure whatever reel you select has a good drag system. Some saltwater fish can strip off 100 yards of line and backing on a single run, so it is important to make sure the drag is smooth and the reel does not vibrate. Also, select a reel that has a drag adjustment mechanism that is convenient to reach, since it may be necessary on occasion to tighten or loosen the tension while playing a fish.

Any reel you invest money in should be designed to take extra spools, too. Even though you may use a floating line much of the time, there will be occasions when a sinking-tip or sinking line will be required. The most practical and least expensive way to get around this is to have an extra spool on hand. Reels capable of taking exchangeable spools are like getting two reels in one and, although you have to buy the extra spool, it is less costly than buying two reels.

Fly reels come in different sizes, of course, with those designed specifically for saltwater use generally falling within two categories: those capable of handling more than 250 yards of line, and those that will hold less than 200 yards. For most inshore fishing, for mackerel, small bluefish, and striped bass, Atlantic salmon, coho salmon, and shad, the smaller reels equipped with 20-pound test backing are fine. Such reels can generally hold up to 200 yards of this line. For some of the larger fish—sharks, large striped bass, monster blues, and big bonito—a reel capable of handling over 200 yards of 25–30 pound test backing plus line is advised. Which size reel you decide to buy should be based on the type of fishing you plan to be doing most. In most cases along the New England coast, one of the medium size reels with at least 200 yards of 20–25 pound test backing will suffice for anything from shad and the salmons to blues and bonito, but, in the long run, one of the larger reels loaded with more backing will allow you to tackle just about anything you desire.

It is also a good idea to check any new reel for sharp edges, especially around the metal guards near the bottom of the reel where the line comes off. Sharp edges or burrs can cut the line, fingers, and hands that may come in contact with them during a battle.

Top row, l to r: Marryat, L.L. Bean Guide Multiplier, L.L. Bean Angler DM; second row: L.L. Bean Double L Salmon, L.L. Bean Double L Bonefish, Billy Pate; third row: STH Eliseos 12, STH Caribbean, Fenwick World Class; bottom row: Valentine 101, Scientific Anglers System 2, Pfleuger Medalist 1495½. (Raychard/Gorham photo)

Some reels have a couple of features which you might want to consider. For example, some reels have an exposed spool rim which allows the angler to "palm" the reel for extra drag. Personally, I like reels with this feature, but they take a little getting used to, and anyone not familiar with such systems may want to experiment on smaller, less powerful freshwater fish before going after saltwater species. Once you get used to palming, however, I think you will discover its advantages, since it allows the angler to assert as much or as little tension as he wants quickly.

Other reels offer an anti-reverse feature, which is a locking system built into the reel allowing the line to be taken out under pressure but preventing the handle from turning. This is a great asset whenever big, powerful fish make long, lightning runs. When the fish suddenly stops, so does the spool, thus preventing the line from becoming tangled into a bird's nest. Fly reels with an anti-reverse feature are often a little more expensive, but are worth the investment. They can also prevent some painful damage to fingers and knuckles, and allow the angler to keep his hands on the handle at all times, which means he can reel in line on a moment's notice.

And finally, any reel to be used a great deal around salt water should be made of corrosion-resistant materials, such as aluminum that has been anodized on the outside and stainless steel, chrome-plated, cadmium-plated, or brass internal parts. Most saltwater reels are, but many freshwater reels we may use in salt water are not. In either case, always make sure to clean your reels (and lines) thoroughly after each use. After detaching the reel from the rod, take it into the house and wash it with warm water and a mild soap or detergent. Cold water will not dissolve all the salt, and using a garden hose only drives the salt, sand, or grit into the reel and its moving parts.

Take the reel apart, making sure to remove all the dirt around the drag system and spindle. If necessary, use a soft brush or toothbrush for hard-to-reach spots. Wipe the reel dry and then give it a light coating of oil or grease and back off the drag adjustment nut so the pressure will not ruin it during storage.

The following are some recommended reels that can be used for saltwater and anadromous fishing:

MAKER	MODEL NUMBER/ REEL NAME	REEL WEIGHT	REEL DIAMETER	LINE CAPACITY
Scientific Anglers	Model 89 System Two	8.1 oz.	N/A	200 yd-20 lb. test plus up WF 9 line
Scientific Anglers	Model 1011 System Two	8.5 oz.	N/A	200 yd-30 lb. test plus up WF 11 line
Orvis	SSS 7/8	$6^{3}/_{4}$ oz.	$3^{1}/_{2}$ in.	200 yd-20 lb. test plus WF 8 line
Orvis	SSS 9/10	$8^{1}/_{2}$ oz.	$3^{3}/_{4}$ in.	200 yd-30 lb. test plus WF 10 line
Orvis	Saltwater CFO	6 oz.	$3^{3}/_{4}$ in.	200 yd-20 lb. test plus WF 9 line
Marryat	MR-8.5	5 oz.	$3^{1}/_{8}$ in.	235 yd-20 lb. test plus WF 8 line
Marryat	MR-9	$5^{1}/_{4}$ oz.	$3^{1}/_{4}$ in.	320 yd-20 lb. test plus WF 9 line
Pflueger Medalist	$1495^{1}/_{2}$	$6^{3}/_{4}$ oz.	$3^{5}/_{8}$ in.	200 yd-20 lb. test plus up WF 11 line
Pfleuger Medalist	1498	$6^{7}/_{8}$ oz.	4 in.	250 yd-20 lb. test plus WF 11 line
Cortland	S Magnum	7.6 oz.	4 in.	325 yd-20 lb. test plus WF 9 line
Fenwick	World Class 2	4.6 oz.	$3^{1}/_{8}$ in.	150 yd-20 lb. test plus WF 6/7 line
Fenwick	World Class 4	6.6 oz.	$3^{1}/_{8}$ in.	200 yd-20 lb. test plus WF 9 line
Fenwick	World Class 6	9.2 oz.	$3^{1}/_{8}$ in.	200 yd-20 lb. test plus WF 9 line

MAKER	MODEL NUMBER/ REEL NAME	REEL WEIGHT	REEL DIAMETER	LINE CAPACITY
Fin-Nor	Standard Series #2	10 3/4 oz.	3 1/8 in.	200 yd-20 lb. test plus WF 9 line
Fin-Nor	Standard Series #3	11 1/2 oz.	3 5/8 in.	450 yd-20 lb. test plus WF 9 line
Fin-Nor	Anti-Reverse Series #3	12 1/2 oz.	3 5/8 in.	200 yd-30 lb. test plus WF 9 line
Fin-Nor	Anti-Reverse Series #4	13 3/4 oz.	3 5/8 in.	450 yd-30 lb. test plus WF 9 line
Hardy	Ocean Prince	11 oz.	3 3/4 in.	350 yd-20 lb. test plus WF 9-10 line
Hardy	St. John	8 1/2 oz.	3 7/8 in.	200 yd-20 lb. test plus WF 7-8 line
Billy Pate	Salmon	8 oz.	3 1/4 in.	200 yd-20 lb. test plus WF 9 line
Valentine	Model 95	6.8 oz.	3 3/4 in.	200 yd-20 lb. test plus WF 9 line
Valentine	Model 101	7.4 oz.	4 in.	300 yd-20 lb. test plus WF 10-11 line
Valentine	Model 375	9 oz.	3 3/4 in.	200 yd-20 lb. test plus WF 9 line
Valentine	Model 400	9 1/2 oz.	4 in.	300 yd-20 lb. test plus WF 10-11 line
L.L. Bean	Double L #6	3 3/4 oz.	3 3/8 in.	110 yd-20 lb. test plus WF 6-7 line
L.L. Bean	Double L #8	3 3/4 oz.	3 3/8 in.	110 yd-20 lb. test plus WF 8-9 line
L.L. Bean	Double L Salmon	6 oz.	3 1/2 in.	220 yd-20 lb. test plus WF 7-8 line
L.L. Bean	Double L Bonefish	6 1/2 oz.	3 3/4 in.	300 yd-20 lb. test plus WF 9-10 line
L.L. Bean	Double L Trophy Tarpon	9 oz.	4 in.	300 yd-20 lb. test plus WF 11-12 line

FLY LINES

Modern fly lines come in a number of sizes, tapers, and densities, and it would appear that any type of line for any purpose the fly fisherman should need is available. Indeed, that is nearly the case. While our angling ancestors had to settle for lines that sank or floated after dressing only, today we can choose from lines that float, sink fast or slow, float and sink, and lines that are level, tapered on both ends, lines that are heavy on the shooting end, and specialty lines that are even heavier on the shooting end. If you fly fish both fresh and salt water you will need a number of these lines, but for salt water and the anadromous species only one or two is required.

The fly line is really an important piece of your fly fishing equipment. It is the fly line that picks up the power from the rod and transmits it to the leader and fly and thus to the target. It also determines whether your offering floats or sinks and, if it does sink, to what depth and how fast or slow it goes. Fly lines are also designed to help make casting flies of certain size easier, come in different sizes or weights to balance a rod, help us reach greater distances, and are important in overall presentation, especially when hitting the water.

There are several things to consider when purchasing a fly line for salt water, and one of the most important is taper. On a trout stream a double-taper line is generally considered the best, but when fishing for brookies, browns, or rainbows, we are casting small flies and wind is not always a problem. On the ocean, however, and even in Atlantic salmon rivers, the weight-forward line has become the standard, since the heavy shooting end helps combat wind and is best capable of handling heavy saltwater flies.

A Weight-Forward Fly Line

A weight-forward fly line is tapered just the way its name implies. Coming off the backing or reel end, the line is level throughout much of its length (running line) but then gets bigger for the last thirty feet forming the head. It is in this head section where most of the line's weight is concentrated and, as you cast, the heavier head or "weight-forward" section easily takes out the lighter belly or running line.

An advantage the fly fisherman has with weight-forward lines is that he can retrieve until only the head section is outside the rod tip, since it can usually be seen or felt. He can then easily and quickly make a single back cast, then a single forward cast shooting the fly back to the target without going through the process of several false casts. Weight-forward lines, because of their heavy shooting end, are the best lines for handling wind conditions and heavy saltwater flies while helping us achieve greater distances with less effort.

There is another type of weight-forward fly line called the saltwater taper. These lines, which are also known as bass-bug tapers, have more weight concentrated in the shooting end than regular weight-forward tapers and were originally designed for distance casting and working large flies into the wind. Although they do offer an advantage for the experienced caster, the novice or person who has trouble casting will find them difficult to work with, simply because these lines have so much weight in their front section that too much energy on the power cast can cause the line to "dump over", creating a poor presentation.

The standard weight-forward line, on the other hand, has a better weight distribution over a greater portion of the line, and the smaller, more delicate taper helps in making better presentations. The standard weight-forward line is also less wind resistant, makes better loops during the cast, and is less likely to dump over on the power stroke. Overall, this is the best taper to go with along the New England and mid-Atlantic coasts and when fishing the anadromous species.

Modern fly lines also come in a number of sizes, from 2 weight all the way up to 11 and 12 weight. Most fly rods today are designed for a specific size line and are generally marked telling the angler what line should be used. The designation is often close to the handle and will read something like, "For #8 Line" or perhaps "AFTMA Line #8," which stands for American Fishing Tackle Manufacturers Association Line #8. Some rods will be marked "AFTMA 6/7" or "AFTMA

7/8" telling the angler that the rod will handle either a 6-weight and 7-weight line, or a 7-weight and 8-weight line, whichever the angler chooses for the type of fishing he will be doing.

For the saltwater fish found along the New England and mid-Atlantic coasts, and for Atlantic salmon, coho salmon, and shad an 8-weight line is perhaps the best. It is by far the most popular among salmon fishermen, and saltwater enthusiasts have found it to be about the best for bluefish, striped bass, and bonito. An 8-weight line is big enough to handle any fish we have, can be delivered without making much disturbance, yet is of the right size to work with for long periods of time. Smaller lines are more apt to be tossed around by the wind and larger lines are simply too big and can be difficult and tiring to cast. Given my choice, I would go with an 8-weight line first, a 7-weight line second, and a 9-weight line third.

The density of a fly line is important, too. As mentioned earlier, there are lines that float, lines that sink at various speeds, and lines that float and sink known as "sink-tips." With most experienced saltwater fly fishermen, the floating line is still the most popular, since it is the most useful and easiest to work with. A floating line is best used when fish are in less than 6 feet of water and, contrary to common belief, can be used with streamers and bucktails as well as surface poppers. If you are a novice fly fisherman or just beginning in salt water, go with a floating line first. It is the best line to learn casting with, and can be used for shad, the salmons, and sea-run trout, as well as for inshore and offshore species.

There will be times, however, when it will be necessary to get the fly down, sometimes down deep and fast. A number of lines can help you accomplish this and which you use is really up to you. I have come to like sinking-tip lines more and more over the years and I have a number of them with tips that sink slow to fast. The floating section makes these lines easy to lift off the water while the sinking portion gets the fly down. Another asset is that, just like the weight-forward taper lines, the angler only has to retrieve the floating section into the tip of the rod. At that point he can usually make a single back cast, then a single forward cast back to the target. With sink-tip lines, in fact, this is generally easier, since the floating and sinking sections are often different colors, and the angler knows when to stop his retrieve.

Whenever fishing the salt, or even when working for Atlantic salmon and coho salmon, I always have a floating and sink-tip line on hand. Which one I use depends on the current conditions, but it is a good idea to have a floater anyway and at least a slow to intermediate sink-tip available. You can start out with just a floating line, but I'm willing to bet you will need a line that will take your fly down before long.

Another fly line that comes in handy at times is the sinking line, even those high-density express lines that have a lead-core lining. Shad and sea-run browns, for example, are often found just off the bottom, and it is necessary many times to get your fly down to their level in a hurry. Sinking lines will also come in handy when striped bass and mackerel are down deep, and they make working fishing reefs and in fast tidal currents possible, which is often necessary when working for shad and coho salmon. In most cases, when it is necessary to get below the surface, I have found a sink-tip will suffice, but if you are serious about saltwater fly fishing, by all means have all three density lines available. If you do, you will be able to tackle any situation. If not, or if you just don't want to invest the money, go with floater and sink-tip.

If you have ever spent some time in a fly shop, it is apparent that fly lines also come in a rainbow of colors these days, from white and tan all the way to fluorescent orange and yellow. I am convinced that fish are spooked more by a fly line flashing overhead than by sloppy presentations, so I have been a student of natural-colored lines whenever fishing shallow water. In these areas, when fish are down ten feet or so below the surface, I feel more confident with a gray, tan or light-green colored line. When fishing deep and at the same level as the fish, I don't think it makes as much difference, but it's a matter of fact in the shallows.

Some fly fishermen, however, feel fly line color below the surface is important, too, and it could very well be. They subscribe to the theory that sinking lines should be dark brown or green, for example, since these colors blend in better with the natural surroundings. I have not experimented enough with sinking lines to make a judgment like I can with floating lines, but to be safe, perhaps it is good to have a natural-colored floating line, perhaps a subtle gray, light to medium green, or light brown, and a dark brown or dark green sink-tip or sinking line. That way you cover all theories and philosophies and should be safe.

It might be helpful for the novice fly fisherman to know how to determine different taper fly lines, sizes, and densities when exploring a fly shop or when ordering from a catalog. In many cases, a clerk or proprietor will lend assistance, but it is always a good idea to know you are getting exactly what you want.

Each fly line box is marked with a code, for example WF-8-F or DT-7-F/S. The first two letters designate the taper of the line: WF means weight-forward, DT means double taper and so on. The number tells you the size of the line—the smaller the number, the smaller the line. The last letter or letters of the code, F for example, tells you it is a floating line, S means sinking, and F/S designates a floating/sinking line or sink tip. The following chart is a list of line tapers and line densities:

DT	**Double Taper**
WF	**Weight Forward**
ST	**Shooting Taper**
L	**Level**
HD	**Sinking/Sink-tip**
F	**Floating**
S	**Sinking**
F/S	**Floating/Sinking or Sink-Tip**
I	**Intermediate Sinking**

BACKING

Fly lines today come in varied lengths, from 80 to more than 100 feet. When fishing for trout we seldom need all the line on the reel, but for saltwater species, Atlantic salmon, and other anadromous species, long runs are common. It is not unusual to experience runs of 150–200 feet or more, which means we need an additional line for insurance. That extra line is known as backing and it is a very important part of your fly fishing outfit.

Several different materials can be used for backing, but braided Dacron® is best. It is supple, very strong, connects to the reel and fly line well, and does not damage rod guides. Another very similar material is Micron®, manufactured by Cortland.

In most cases, 150 yards of 20–25 pound test line is considered minimum for saltwater fly fishing (and when fishing for anadromous species). Many fishermen prefer at least 200 yards—maybe even 250–300 yards. 30-pound test line is also used, especially for the larger offshore species, but along the New England coast I don't really think it is necessary. When I fish, I use 200 yards of 25-pound test Dacron, and use it on everything from Atlantic salmon to bonito with no problems. It is always a good idea to have excess backing, perhaps 250 yards, than not enough.

There are several ways of attaching backing to a fly reel. If you have a large fish on, who is capable of taking out all your fly line and backing down to the hub, no knot is going to hold him, so knot strength is not overly critical. You do want a knot that will hold to a point, however, and an easy way of doing it is as follows:

Step 1—Tie a simple knot in the end of the braided line and insert the line around the hub of the reel.

Step 2—With the tag end, tie a simple overhand knot around the mainline or standing line.

Step 3—Tighten the overhand knot by pulling on the tag end and mainline. Once the knot has been tightened, pull on the mainline part and the knot will slide securely up against the hub. Trim any excess line making sure to leave the knot on the tag end.

Tying the backing to the fly line is more important, since it is very likely you will get down to this point at some time when playing big fish. It can be done by using a Nail Knot or Needle Nail Knot (see Chapter 4). Both are excellent knots for this purpose.

Chapter 4

LEADERS, KNOTS, AND LOOPS

Some very important, yet misunderstood and largely taken for granted, elements of saltwater fly fishing are leaders and connectors. Most of us who fly fish seem to put the emphasis on rods, reels, lines, flies, etc.—while the truth of the matter is that none of that fancy stuff will work the way it's supposed to without the right leader material at the business end, and without everything tied together with the right knots and loops. Actually, the knots are far and away the most important, since you'll never even get a line into the water without 'em! Loops are really just glorified knots, but they deserve, and get, a small section to themselves in this chapter. After all, they've got to be right, too!

LEADERS

Many fly fishermen consider a leader nothing more than a transparent connection between fly line and fly; theoretically, they're right. A great many more believe that a long leader is always best; maybe in fresh water for trout and salmon, but reserve your judgment about saltwater leaders for a bit.

Although there are practically as many theories about how to rig and use a leader as there are fishermen, one thing seems to emerge as the real truth—it isn't **what** you use, but **how** you use it, especially in saltwater fly fishing.

LONG LEADERS

Let's start right out with the facts—most of the time, I rely on a leader between 6 and 8 feet long, unless a specific situation says "No!" I use this length leader simply because I feel comfortable with it and can make the delicate presentations required to catch fish with it. That's the key—if you can make it work, it's the right one for you!

The problem with leaders of more than 6 or 7 feet in length is primarily that they are harder to handle than shorter ones, giving room for a number of casting errors and sloppy presentations. Even the experts get tired—but one sloppy cast is all it takes to alert the fish in the neighborhood that "Ole Dubber is here!" Be sure you can handle a long leader—practice before trying one out on a stream full of trout during a record hatch!

Another big problem with long leaders is wind. It is much more difficult to cast into the wind with a long leader, and Atlantic saltwater casting involves a lot of "into-the-wind" activity. If it's windy, switch to a shorter leader right away. You'll be happier at day's end!

Long leaders also tend to sink less quickly than short leaders. So flies on long leaders sink more slowly, and you might just miss a fish on the move because the fly didn't get down far or quickly enough.

SHORT LEADERS

What can I say? I really don't mind using shorter leaders for saltwater fly fishing, since I am convinced that a) the length of the leader is not really as important as your technique, and b) it is easier to put the fly where you want it with a shorter leader. As you gain experience, the situation will dictate whether you use short or long leaders, but try this for starters: if the weather isn't a factor, use between 6 and 8 feet

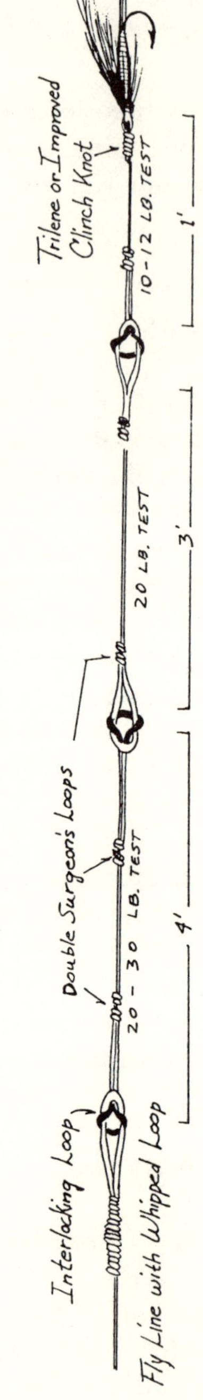

Standard Long Leader

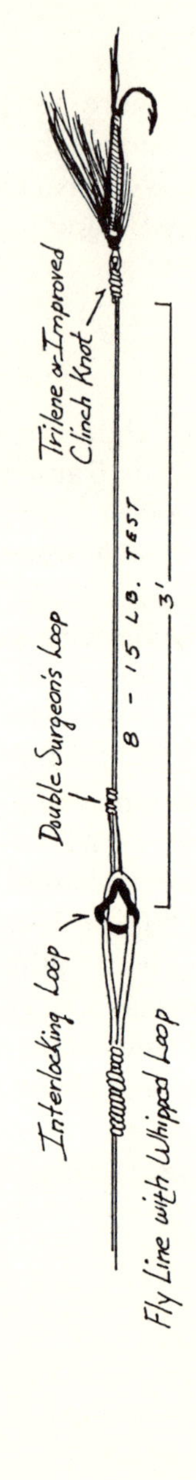

Standard Short Leader

of leader; less if it's windy, more if you feel you can handle it. Experiment!

The illustrations on page 84 show my "standards" for saltwater fishing on the New England coast. Observe the following: short leaders (under 3 feet) are one material only; longer leaders are made up of several different materials; I use loop-to-loop connections whenever possible, because I like them, but knots probably work just as well.

SHOCK TIPPETS

I have recently been experimenting with bluefish and other heavier, sharp-toothed species, trying to land them **without** using wire next to the fly. I was pleased when Nylostrand® came along (see **TYPES OF LEADER MATERIAL**, below), since I don't really like using wire. But another technique, or type of rig, has proven itself quite adept at handling big fish, maintaining some resistance to their sharp teeth and to the rocky bottoms of their habitats, while still allowing good presentations. It is a shock tippet.

This method has been around for a long time, and is quite easy to rig. It is really nothing more than a section of **heavy** monofilament, I mean **heavy** (from 50- to 100-pound test), connected to the business end of your leader. This heavier piece of monofilament is then attached directly to the fly, using a 3½ Turn Clinch Knot. The rig is extremely strong, and acts somewhat like a shooting head because of its extra weight.

To connect the smaller line to the shock tippet, use the Improved Blood Knot (p. 101). The knot may sound a bit complicated to tie, but you'll get the hang of it!

TYPES OF LEADER MATERIAL

MONOFILAMENT. There are several reasons why monofilament is the leader choice of the overwhelming majority of fishermen. It is easy to tie knots in monofilament, or to construct loops; it is transparent (or close to it); it can be purchased in various strengths, and is extremely strong when used properly. Drawbacks, however, are as follows: it is easily cut (for instance, by the sharp teeth of fighting fish such as bluefish, king mackerel, and sharks), and not every knot will hold in monofilament (don't, for instance, use an Improved Clinch Knot with monofilament over 40-pound test, although it works wonderfully with smaller weights of the same line).

Monofilament not only comes in many strengths, but in several different "stiffnesses"—from limp to very stiff. Limp mono is not a good choice for saltwater fishing, because it doesn't hold knots well and stretches too much, making it difficult to set a hook. Stiff mono, on the other hand, is susceptible to breaking because it has very little "give" to it.

The "middle-of-the-road" rule applies here—a medium-strength, medium-stiff monofilament is a good leader material to choose. Some stretch, some strength, some resistance to cutting, some holding power for knots—it's an averaging process! The important thing to remember when purchasing monofilament is not to skimp on quality. Buy a brand that's been recommended to you, or one you recognize from your own experience. Pay more for it, but expect your money's worth. You won't be disappointed.

Wire. There are essentially two types of wire leader available: solid and braided. There are advantages and disadvantages to each.

Solid wire has a smaller diameter than equivalent strength braided wire, and is therefore easier to cast—but its lack of "give" and tendency towards kinking make it more difficult to tie into effective knots.

Braided wire, although much easier to tie and much less susceptible to kinking, is much larger in diameter—enough to significantly affect casting. Also, it has a tendency to fray when confronted with repeated attacks from sharp teeth, making frequent changes necessary. It is available coated with nylon, which some feel makes it easier to cast, but nylon-coated braided wire is nearly twice the diameter of solid wire, making casting much more difficult.

I personally prefer braided wire, and I have learned to accept the added difficulty in casting—but I **do** keep a sharp eye for fraying, and make the necessary changes before the line is unduly weakened, or frayed beyond the point where it can be effectively cast.

Nylostrand®. This material is neat! It has an inner core of braided stainless steel wire, covered by a special nylon which is harder than that found on other covered wire. It is available in pound ratings from 15 to 210; it looks a lot like fly line, and can be easily cast.

Another really great thing about Nylostrand is that the nylon covering can be melted together with a match or lighter. Once cooled, this creates a solid nylon covering over a knot or other connection, a very strong and weather-resistant joint. I rarely tie a knot in Nylostrand, actually; I simply feed one end through the loop on the previous line segment, twist the end around the standing part five or six times, then melt it together. I can then do the same thing at the other end, feeding the line through the eye of the hook and around the standing part and melting the whole thing together. I have **never** had one of these connections break, even when fighting bluefish! (Note: It is important to connect the Nylostrand to the next **line** segment first, then make your connection to the **fly**.)

KNOTS

There are a few things to remember when tying any knot. First, always lubricate the knot with saliva before pulling it tight. Next, make sure the knot is tightened with a steady, continuous pull—**don't jerk it!** It may be necessary, when pulling a knot tight, to wear gloves to protect your hands. Finally, trim the tag ends of knots and loops, using a pair of small scissors or nail clippers. This will prevent a possible snag when the knot runs through your rod guides, and prevent the knot from picking up debris in the water. Some knots could even benefit from a drop or two of cement, which helps set the knot and prevent loose ends from snagging.

Once the knot is formed, exert one or two steady pulls to check it. Better it should come apart now, in your hands, than later, in the lunker's mouth!

FOR TYING MONOFILAMENT TO FLIES:

Improved Clinch Knot. Used with lines up to 40-pound test, this is the most popular knot for this purpose. The important thing here is the number of turns around the standing part—five is the number, less reducing the knot's strength and more making it impossible to seat and tighten the knot correctly.

Step 1—Insert the end through the eye of the hook, leaving six to eight inches of line with which to tie the knot.

Step 2—Hold the fly between the thumb and forefinger; with the other hand, take the tag end five times around the standing part.

Step 3—Bring the tag end down and through the loop of line right next to the hook's eye.

Step 4—Now take the end back through the loop which was formed by Step 3.

Step 5—Moisten the knot, pull steadily to tighten, then trim.

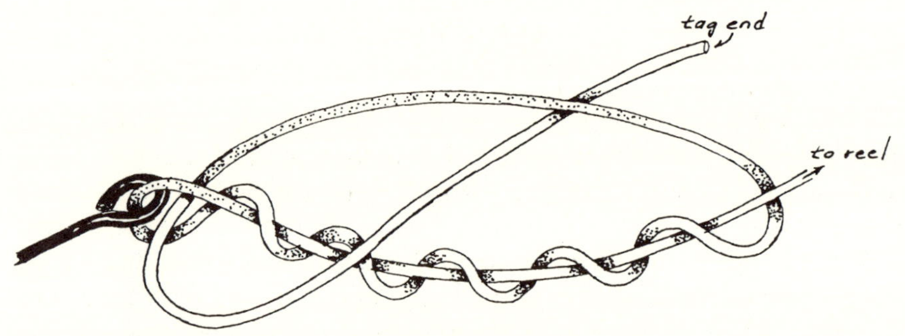

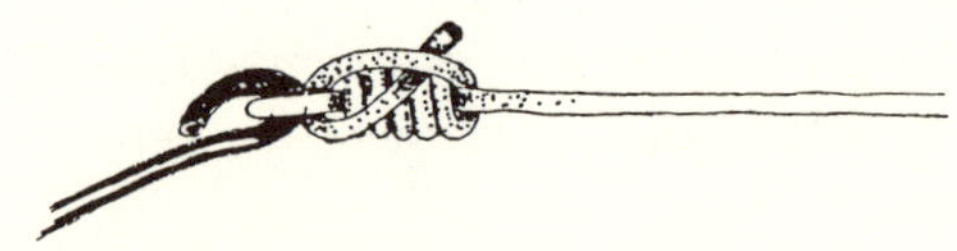

Improved Clinch Knot

3½ Turn Clinch Knot. Best used with heavier lines (over 20-pound test), this differs from the previous knot in two ways: only three and one-half turns are taken in Step 2, and Step 4 is eliminated altogether. In Step 5, it is wise to hold the hook with pliers and wear a glove on your other hand when tightening the knot in heavier monofilament.

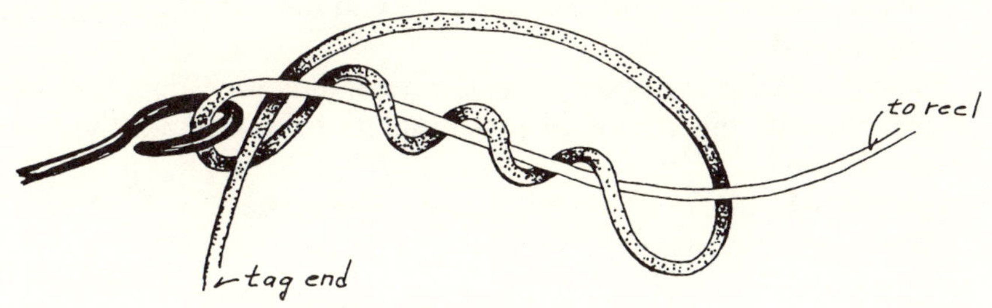

3½ Turn Clinch Knot

TRILENE KNOT. In 1985, while waiting in Chicago for a connecting flight to Alaska, I bumped into Lefty Kreh, one of the world's great fly fishing technicians. He showed me this knot, and I have used it ever since. It can be tied in nearly all weights of monofilament, and is, when tied correctly, the **strongest** knot for single-strand monofilament.

Step 1—Insert the tag end through the eye of the fly, leaving six to eight inches with which to tie the knot.

Step 2—Circle around and insert the end through the eye again, making a double loop.

Step 3—Make five wraps around the standing part, then feed the end through the double loop. **Do not** go back through the loop just formed.

Step 4—Lubricate the knot, tighten, then trim.

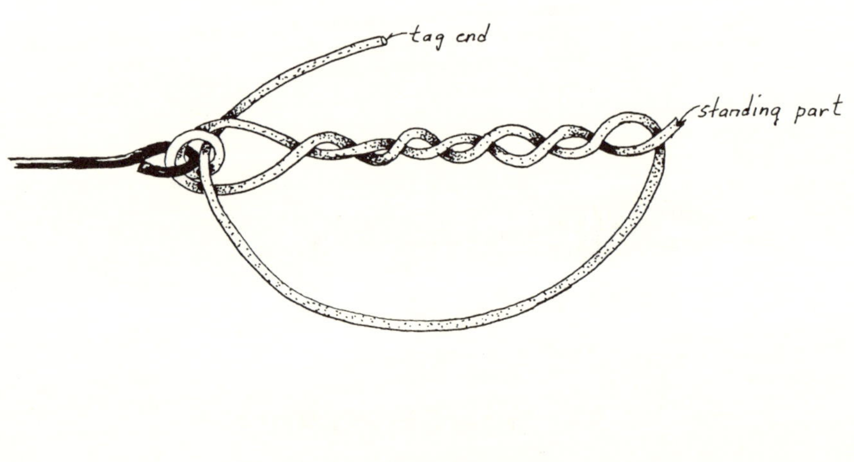

Trilene Knot

PALOMAR KNOT. Another easy one to tie, the Palomar can be used with fairly heavy lines and provides nearly 100% breaking strength when correctly tied.

Step 1—Double the tag end back against the standing part, then feed the resulting loop through the eye of the fly, leaving six to eight inches with which to tie the knot.

Step 2—Tie a standard overhand knot, making sure the loop you form faces the bend in the hook. **DO NOT TIGHTEN THIS OVERHAND KNOT!**

Step 3—Slip the loop formed by the overhand knot over the hook, making sure to hold the overhand knot in place.

Step 4—Hold the hook with pliers, moisten and tighten the knot, then trim.

Palomar Knot

FOR TYING WIRE TO FLIES:

Homer Rhode Loop Knot. This knot can be quite quickly and easily tied, and works well with monofilament and plastic-coated braided wire lines. It has a fairly low breaking point, and should therefore be used only with larger lines, but the knot forms a small loop next to the eye, allowing freedom of hook movement which often will entice a fish that would not otherwise have looked twice at your offering.

Step 1—Form a simple overhand knot near the end of the line, leaving about four or five inches of tag extending past the loop.

Step 2—Insert the tag end through the eye of the hook.

Step 3—Pass the tag end through the loop formed by the overhand knot.

Step 4—Hold the fly in one hand and pull standing part and tag end together to close the overhand knot.

Step 5—Release the standing part and pull on the tag end to slide the overhand knot down to the eye of the hook.

Step 6—Form another overhand knot around the standing part with what is left of the tag end; grasp the tag end with pliers and pull the second overhand up next to the first; trim.

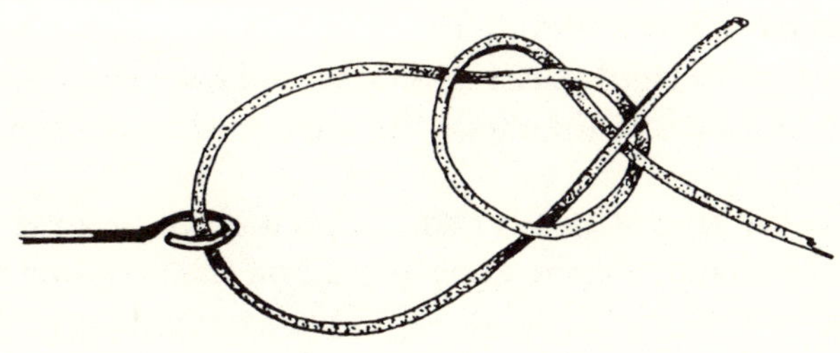

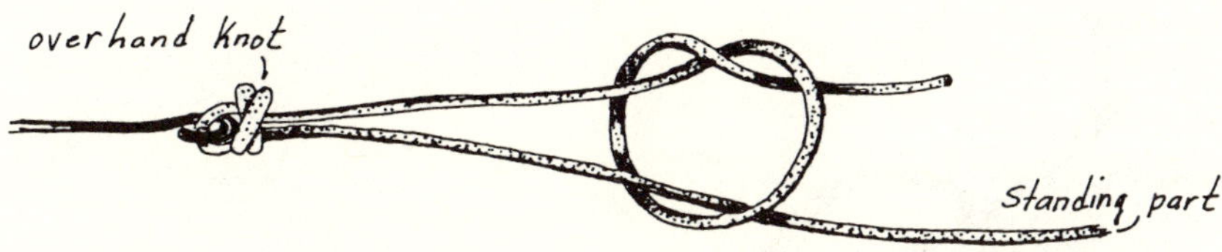

Homer Rhode Loop Knot

FIGURE 8 KNOT. This is a quick and strong method of tying **braided wire** to a fly. Breaking strength is very high when tied properly.

Step 1—Insert the tag end through the eye of the hook, bringing it back and **under** the standing part.

Step 2—Continue around, passing the tag end over the standing part to form a "Figure 8", then pass the tag end through the loop next to the eye.

Step 3—Hold the fly with pliers and, with a glove or a rag protecting the other hand, set the knot by pulling the standing part. Trim, making sure to leave 1/16″ to 1/8″ of wire extending past the knot.

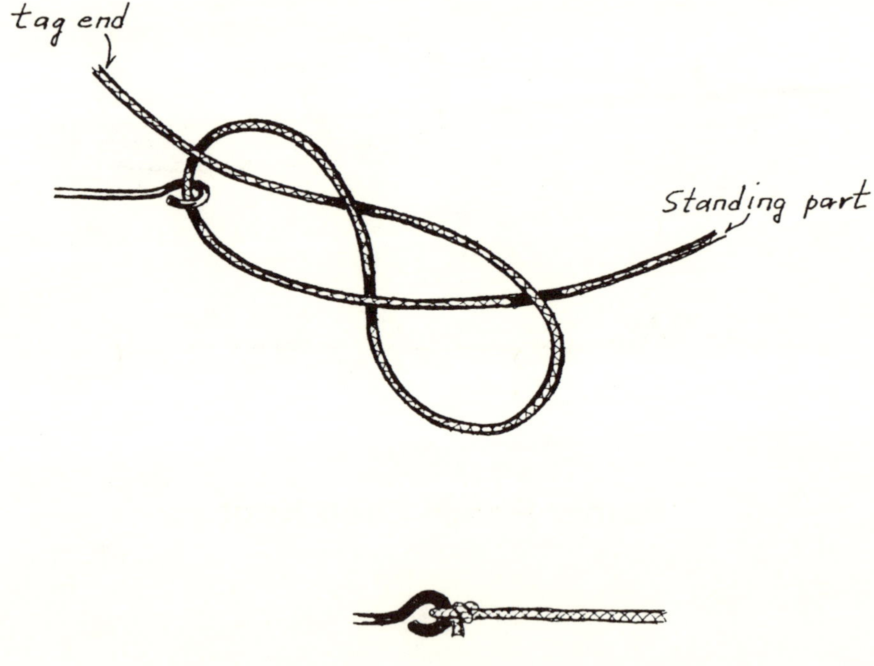

Figure 8 Knot

HEATED TWIST. This is perhaps the quickest way to attach plastic or nylon-coated wire (including Nylostrand) to a fly. It's very strong when correctly tied.

Step 1—Insert the tag end through the eye of the hook and bring it around the standing part four or five times, making sure that it doesn't unravel.

Step 2—Heat the plastic, using a match or lighter (no additional heat is needed). Hold the heat source at least one inch below the line, and make sure not to burn the covering away.

Step 3—When sufficiently melted together, allow it to cool, then trim if necessary (there shouldn't be much trimming to do!).

Heated Twist

Haywire Twist. This is a very good, very strong way to attach a fly to solid wire.

Step 1—Insert the tag end through the eye of the hook, leaving five or six inches of line with which to tie the knot.

Step 2—Bend the tag end over the standing part in such a way as to form a **small** loop next to the eye.

Step 3—With tag end in one hand and standing part in the other, twist them together three or four times, forming an "X" each time (by which I mean to make sure that both parts move—don't just twist the tag around the standing part).

Step 4—After you've made your "X" wraps, bend the tag end to a right angle with the standing part, then wrap the tag end around the standing part three or four times, making sure the wraps are tight around the line and very close together. Then bend the excess wire back and forth until it breaks off (never cut solid wire, as it will leave a sharp burr which can cause injury).

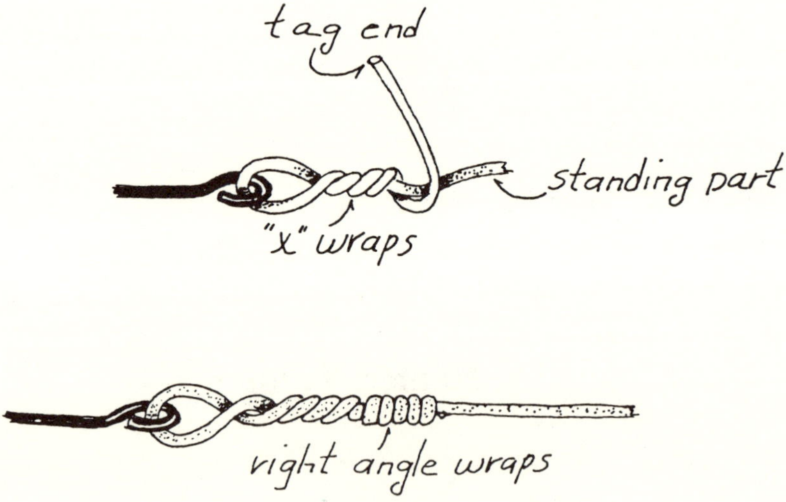

tag end

standing part

"X" wraps

right angle wraps

Haywire Twist

FOR TYING WIRE AND LEAD-CORE TO MONOFILAMENT:

Modified Nail Knot. This is the best way I know for connecting lead-core line to monofilament. It takes a bit of practice to master, and you need a nail, needle, or (what I prefer to use) the filler from a ball point pen.

Step 1—Lay the tool (be it nail, needle, or tube) on top of the lead-core line, then place the monofilament on top of the tube (stack them right up—lead-core on the bottom going left to right, monofilament on top going right to left), leaving eight to ten inches of monofilament with which to tie the knot.

Step 2—Make three wraps around both tube and lead-core with the monofilament, keeping the wraps as close together and tight as possible.

Step 3—Lift the tag end **of the lead-core** back out of the way and make another wrap around the tube.

Step 4—Lay the lead-core back into position and make three more wraps with the monofilament.

Step 5—Insert the tag end of the monofilament through the tube (or next to the nail or needle) until it passes under all the wraps, then SLOWLY remove the tool, pulling it towards the tag end of the monofilament.

Step 6—Pinch the knot between thumb and forefinger; pull first the tag end of the monofilament, then the standing part, to tighten the knot. Trim.

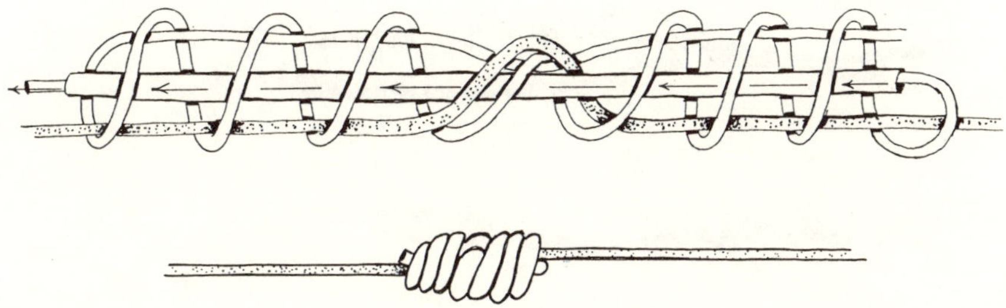

Modified Nail Knot

ALBRIGHT KNOT. This is perhaps the best knot for connecting monofilament to solid wire. Like other knots designed for this purpose, it alleviates the problem of the wire cutting the monofilament under stress (but it doesn't eliminate it altogether).

Step 1—Make a Haywire Twist in one end of the wire and elongate the loop.

Step 2—Insert the tag end of the monofilament through the wire loop, leaving 12 to 16 inches of line with which to tie the knot.

Step 3—With the tag end in one hand and the loop in the other, bring the tag end forward (towards the rounded part of the loop) and around the loop, making sure that this wrap crosses the monofilament coming through the loop.

Step 4—Continue to wrap forward, keeping the wraps tight and close together, at least 10 more turns; when you have completed the wraps, insert the tag end back through the loop, making sure it comes out the same way it originally went in. It may be necessary to hold the wraps in place during this step.

Step 5—Continuing to hold the wraps in place, push them forward to within 1/8″ of the loop end.

Step 6—This knot must be tightened **slowly**. Grasp the tag end of the monofilament with pliers and pull it tight FIRST, while holding the standing part. Then pull on the standing part. Repeat the pulls, alternating between tag end and standing part, until the loop closes.

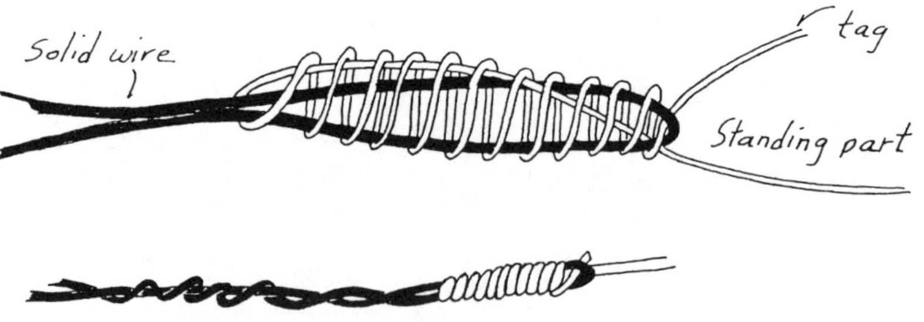

Albright Knot

OTHER USEFUL KNOTS:

NAIL KNOT. This knot differs from the Modified Nail Knot above in only one way: eliminate **Step 3** (the extra wrap with the line pulled back) and combine **Step 2** and **Step 4**, making six tight wraps around the joint. The extra wrap gives the Modified Nail Knot some extra strength when connecting lead-core line to monofilament, but the regular Nail Knot is fine for connecting a leader or permanent butt section to a fly line.

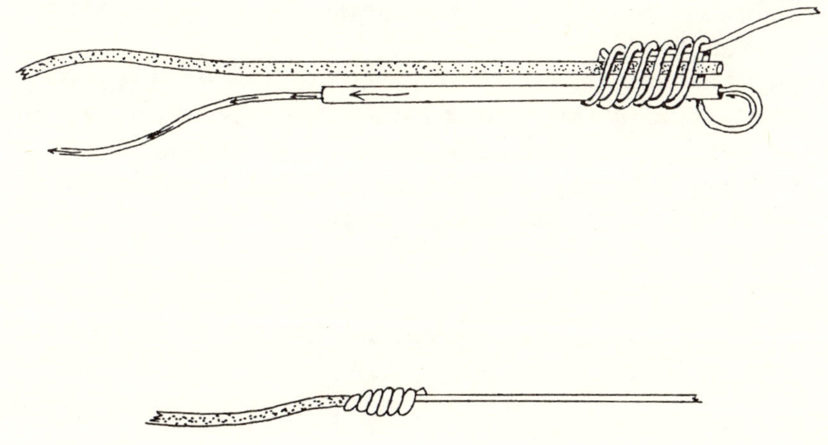

Nail Knot

Needle Nail Knot. This knot is the best way to connect a leader or butt section to a fly line, not only because of its strength but because the leader flows from the **center** of the fly line.

Step 1—Holding the monofilament down on a hard surface with one hand, position a razor blade over the line at a 45° angle towards the tag end. Pull the monofilament slowly to form a very sharp point. This may seem difficult at first, but keep at it!

Step 2—Insert the end of the mono through the eye of a needle, assuming you have already found a needle with an eye of sufficient size.

Step 3—Insert the needle into the center of your fly line, working it up in from the end, then out through the side about 1/4″ to 1/2″ from the end.

Step 4—Grasp the end of the needle with pliers; hold the fly line between thumb and forefinger and pull the needle and monofilament through the fly line and out through the side.

Step 5—Pull enough monofilament through the fly line to tie a Nail Knot, then tie one around the fly line. Trim.

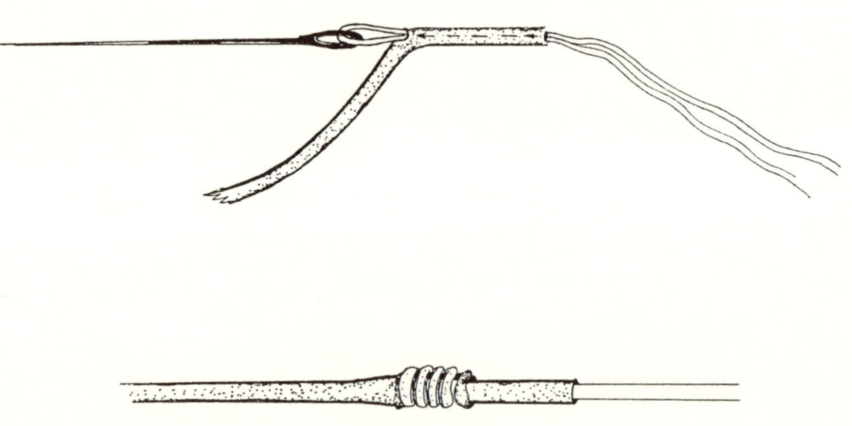

Needle Nail Knot

Improved Blood Knot. This knot excels at connecting the heavy monofilament of a shock tippet to the adjacent lighter leader material. Two things must be remembered—double the smaller line, and always take more wraps with the smaller than with the larger. Trust me!

Step 1—Double the smaller line, laying the tag end against the standing part; lay this small line over the larger line to form an "X".

Step 2—Take the smaller, doubled line and make six wraps around the larger line.

Step 3—Make three wraps around the smaller line with the larger line.

Step 4—Take the tag ends of both lines and insert them through the opening where they were first crossed (there **should be** a small opening there). One end should go through from top to bottom, the other from bottom to top.

Step 5—Moisten the knot, then tighten the Improved Blood Knot with a **sharp** jerk on BOTH standing lines (a real exception to the rule!). Trim.

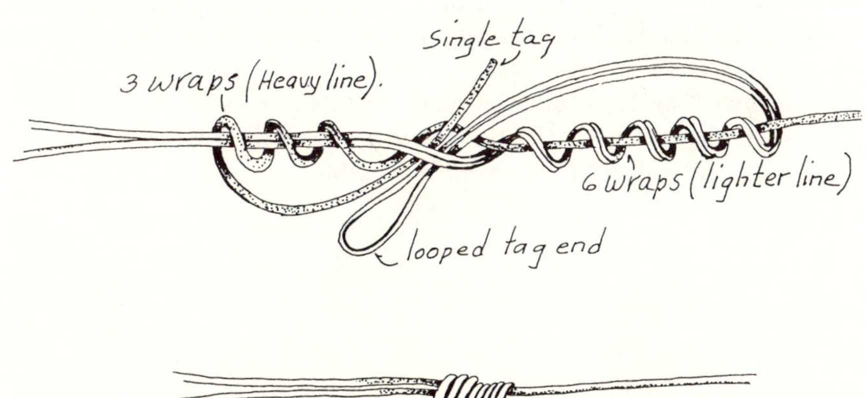

Improved Blood Knot

LOOPS

Loops are extremely useful additions to the fly fisherman's tying "repertoire." I have come to rely on them a great deal over the years, since they are easy to tie, allow fast changes of line and leader, and are very strong connections. I have yet to lose a fish due to a failed loop.

LOOPING A FLY LINE. If you decide to use loops rather than knots, you will need a permanent loop in the end of your fly line. Here's one good way to do it.

Step 1—Cut the tag end of your fly line on an angle, using a razor blade (as in the Needle Nail Knot, above). Then lay the tag end on the standing part to form a loop.

Step 2—Using a bobbin (just like those used in tying flies) loaded with size A thread, wrap the tag end and standing part together as you would when winding a rod guide or whipping rope ends. Make sure to keep tension on the thread; attempt to "bury" the thread in the fly line coating, at least on your initial wraps. Build the wrap towards the loop and back, covering an area of approximately 1/2″ and keeping the wraps TIGHT! When you have completed the wrap, tie the thread off with a whip finish, then paint with head cement for a durable weatherproof coating.

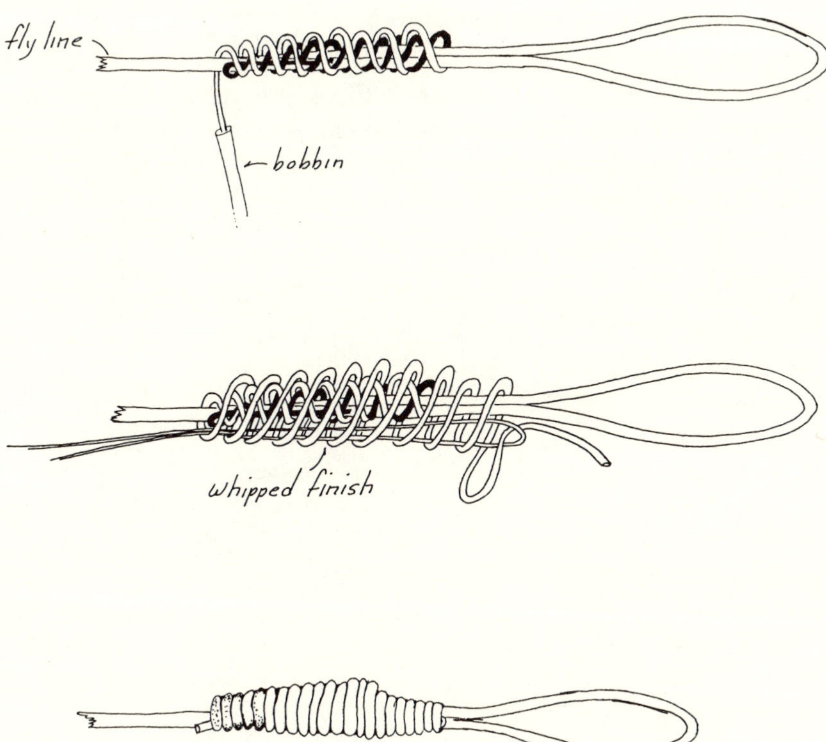

Looping a Fly Line

Double Surgeon's Knot. This is the easiest and strongest loop knot to make, so why try to improve on it by listing several others?

Step 1—Double over the tag end of the monofilament line, then make a simple overhand knot in the doubled line. DO NOT TIGHTEN.

Step 2—Insert the loop through the overhand knot just made.

Step 3—Moisten the knot; hold the loop in one hand and the tag end **and** standing part of the monofilament in the other and pull to tighten. Trim.

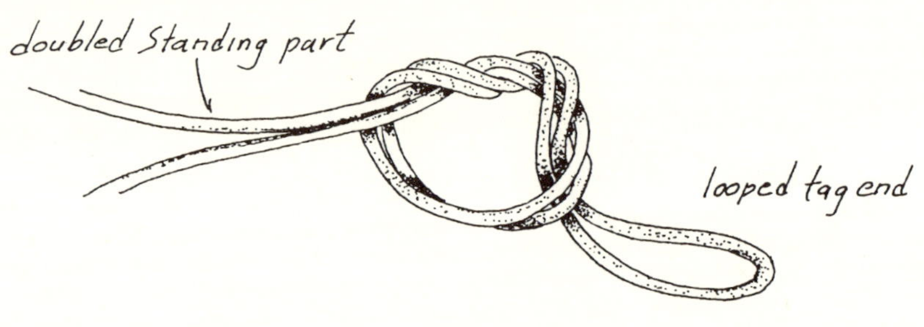

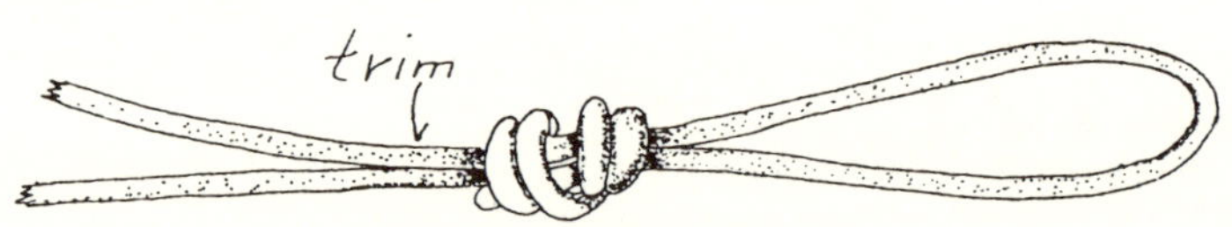

Double Surgeon's Knot

Many other knots and loops (literally thousands) are available to the fisherman. A good resource for more of them is *Practical Fishing Knots* by Lefty Kreh and Mark Sosin, published by Winchester Press. Ask for it at your local bookstore.

Chapter 5

TIDES, CASTING, AND TECHNIQUES

TIDES

One of the first things I discovered about fly fishing in salt water is that tides play a major role in success. It is a common misconception that fish are found scattered throughout the ocean and, because of their abundance, action is possible simply by going out and casting a fly. This is hardly the case.

Just as trout and salmon in a river or stream are influenced by current and water flow, bluefish, striped bass, and other saltwater species are influenced by tides. Understanding how tides control movement of the fish upon which the larger species feed will not only show how important baitfish are to the larger individuals, but will also increase your chances of success.

Keep in mind that baitfish in the salt or a coastal river do not have any specific home or holding area. In most cases, they are too small to fight the power of incoming and outgoing tides, and therefore, may be in a certain area one day, or part of a day, and gone the next. Many species simply ride the tides. The large predator fish we seek with a fly rod know this, of course, and generally lie in wait, attacking the baitfish when the tides make them most vulnerable.

This is the main reason why some of the best saltwater action is found around schools of small baitfish. Whenever you locate such a school, chances are good that one of the larger species is not far away, and your chance for success is good. The important thing to remember is to approach carefully, never driving your boat into the middle of the school. Station your craft on the outside of the school and either cast into it or along its edges. The same is true when wading. If you see a school of baitfish hugging the shoreline of a bay or tidal river, approach as close as you can without spooking it and cast to its outer edges or into the middle, working your fly into the open water.

If I had my choice, I would most often fish on a low tide or outgoing tide, especially in bays and river mouth areas. When the water is low, baitfish will try to hold in deep channels, pools, next to shorelines and breakwaters, for example, until forced to move. Because of decreasing water levels, fish are concentrated in specific areas, giving the angler an advantage when deciding where to devote his efforts. River mouths, narrow channels, and guts can be especially productive on the outgoing tide, since baitfish must pass through these areas, and predators will usually hold along the edges, taking advantage of the situation as baitfish are flushed through.

I also like the outgoing tide because many river mouths have deep trenches, ditches, and mainstream areas, through which baitfish and larger game must travel to reach the open sea. Again, baitfish will try to hold to the shallows as long as they can, but, in the end, they will be forced to leave as the tide recedes, and it is these deep water areas that they will have to utilize. The larger fish know this, and will often establish feeding lanes or stations in these areas, having a field day as the baitfish move out.

It is always important to remember that tides daily force baitfish from one location to the next, and that the larger predators know this and take advantage of the situation. What is equally important, from an angling point of view, is to fish those areas where common sense suggests baitfish are most abundant and vulnerable during the period you are on the water. Remember, you have to hunt these fish, and blind-casting pays no big dividends here.

Tides also influence water temperatures and, believe it or not, saltwater fish are as fussy about temperature as freshwater fish. Bluefish, striped bass, and bonito all have a preferred temperature range and will not come in close until that point is reached. On the other extreme, if a river is too warm some of the best action will be found where waters are cooler.

Actually, the saltwater fly fisherman doesn't have to worry a great deal about water temperature. The waters along our coast remain fairly comfortable throughout the spring, summer, and fall seasons, as do the majority of our bays and coastal rivers. However, you will learn in time that striped bass will not be found off the coast of Maine until late May or early June, when ocean temperatures have started to warm, and they will disappear by mid-September or early October when the currents turn cold again. This is a prime example of how water temperature influences saltwater fish, and it is something which should be kept in mind.

Remember, too, that shallow bays and small rivers heat up more quickly than larger areas under the summer sun, and therefore may not produce the action one might expect. In these areas, fishing the incoming tide is sometimes best, since the tide brings cooler water with it, along with baitfish, and the larger predators are not far away.

Another type of habitat that is best fished on the incoming tides is bays or rivers with a grass bottom. When the water is low, the vegetation absorbs the heat of the sun, thus warming water temperatures. When the tide turns, however, cooler water is flushed in, and with the presence of baitfish, the fish we want to tackle on a fly rod will follow.

Common sense plays a major role when it comes to when and where to fish a particular tide. Each fisherman has his preferred time, and as you develop more experience, you will undoubtedly find yours. However, keep in mind the importance of baitfish and how the tides control their movement and positioning. Baitfish availability, abundance, and vulnerability are keys to saltwater fly fishing success.

You will also learn that several saltwater species which are often found in the shallows and close to the surface (striped bass, for example) will often congregate in the same areas of a bay or river year after year unless there is some kind of change during the spring run-off. Once you get to know the area and which tide is best for fishing, there will be less chance of miscalculation. The real test comes when you explore new or unfamiliar waters, but even then, common sense and

(Raychard photo)

some pre-casting exploration can make a big difference.

But if you are unsure about a certain area, it often pays to invest in the services of a good guide or charter boat for a day. If you do not want to go that route, take the time to check with local tackle and bait shops in the vicinity. The proprietors of these establishments are often fishermen themselves, and are generally willing to offer advice. They can tell you which tide produces the best action and suggest some other productive areas, too. I have the telephone numbers of several dozen such shops up and down the coast. When I want to know how the action is, I simply make a call, ask how things look and on which tide things are happening; I plan my visit accordingly. Some shopkeepers will even tell you at what time of day a particular tide will take place in their areas, which is often a big help.

In your local area, tide tables are usually offered in town or city newspapers, on the radio, and the evening news. During the saltwater fishing season I pay as much attention to that information and the extended weather forecast as I do to sports or the general news. It's important that you know your area well, for it suggests where you should be at a certain time on the day you plan to fish.

PREPARING TO CAST

The art of casting to and catching saltwater fish is an entirely different world from anything normally experienced in fresh water. The same is true with the anadromous species, although some freshwater tactics come into play in this area. In either case, stalking the prize is necessary more times than not, the fish are bigger and more powerful, demanding more respect, the fishing conditions and environs are different, and, in most cases, more patience and tact are required. It is also necessary to take several things into consideration, including wading and boating practices and casting technique.

Ninety percent of your saltwater fishing will be done from a boat, with the rest of your time spent working from breakwaters, jetties, and piers, or by wading. It is important, therefore, that your craft be properly prepared and used as efficiently as your other gear, so that casting and playing fish becomes much easier, and there is less chance of getting line snarled on loose equipment.

First of all, the ideal saltwater boat for fly fishing is one with a flat forward deck which gives the angler a solid base from which to cast. I have fished out of several bass boats, the type that have become quite popular in recent years, and I think they are among the best things going. They are not designed for long runs offshore, but in large bays and rivers they can handle just about anything.

If you do not have such a boat or access to one, most small to medium size boats can be easily equipped for saltwater casting. Cut a piece of 1/2-inch or 3/4-inch plywood 3 1/2 feet by 3 1/2 feet square. Using some steel brackets bent to 90° angles and a few wood and metal screws, the platform can be secured to the bow providing a solid casting base.

An easier way to overcome this problem, however, is by using a "shooting basket". Most fly fishermen can work from a boat with a "V"

(Raychard photo)

bottom, but the main problem is getting line tangled around oars, anchors, and nets. A shooting basket eliminates this problem. Basically, all you need is a small plastic waste basket positioned in front of you at your feet. All excess line is fed into the basket as it is retrieved, which keeps the line free and readily available.

Similarly, a smaller shooting basket can be used when wading or when fishing from shore or rock breakwaters and jetties. Sand can damage lines and reels, and rocks can easily cut a line, especially if it catches on the power stroke. (I have done it more than once!) Shooting baskets which can be worn around the waist can be purchased at many tackle and fly shops but, to tell you the truth, I have found that a small cardboard box or plastic gallon milk jug cut off just above the handle works fine. They also help keep line up out of the water when wading tidal rivers where grass and floating debris are often a problem.

The important thing, of course, is to remove any line-catching gadgets that might be in your way. This would include oars, anchors, nets, tackle boxes, and the like. Give yourself plenty of room in which to work. If you have 50 feet of line sprawled out on the deck when making a cast or when a big fish hits, you'll be glad you did.

Once the angler has eliminated his line problems, he can actually begin casting. In almost all cases, I have found it best to strip off line from the reel before making a cast, laying the line in the basket or on the deck. You will notice many lines may remain in tight loops even after you strip them from the reel. This is caused by line "memory", a term used to describe the action of the nylon inner core of the line, which has a tendency to remain in the position it was last stored. You should eliminate this characteristic before casting by giving the line a steady pull, just as you might straighten out a heavy leader.

You should also check your drag before making your initial cast. Keep in mind that, unlike freshwater fishing, you will battle saltwater and anadromous adversaries from the reel, making proper drag extremely important. There is no sure-fire way of pre-setting a drag prior to hooking a fish since each is different. It is something that develops with time and trial and error. After some experimenting you'll get the "touch" and have a good idea where the drag should be set.

As a general rule of thumb, it is best to have the drag set light rather than heavy, since a sudden surge with a tight drag may cause a break-off. You should also familiarize yourself with the fine-tuning of your drag system. Knowing where the drag button or screw is so you can get to it quickly will prove highly beneficial during a battle, when your mind is on the fish at the end of the line and an adjustment is necessary.

CASTING TECHNIQUES

MAKING THE LONG-DISTANCE CAST

One problem many fly fishermen accustomed to fresh water have when they start out on saltwater species is casting. When fishing a stream or pond casts of under 40 feet are the general rule. On the salt such a distance is considered short. In many situations it is necessary to throw a fly from 70 to 80 or even 100 feet for cruising striped bass.

This is also true with bonito in most cases, so it is imperative to fine tune your casting ability to the point where long distance casts can be made easily.

Depending upon the species you are seeking and the type of water you are working, it is also important to throw your fly fast and accurately. This is especially true when fish are working the surface and when casting to fish in the shallows. In these two situations getting your fly to the fish, or to a point where he will cruise into it quickly, often within a matter of seconds, and being on target are essential to success. There simply isn't enough time for a series of false casts, for by the time you get enough line out, chances are that the fish will have gone down or traveled out of range.

There is also the wind to contend with; I dare say, sea-breeze gives fly fishermen more headaches than anything else. Except on rare summer days, wind is a constant companion, something the saltwater fly fisherman must live with, and learn how to work in, if he is to be successful. There are, however, certain basic rules which you can follow, and a few easy techniques you can practice to help obtain long distance casts more easily and to help combat the wind.

As mentioned previously, always start with at least half of your fly line lying on the deck or in a shooting basket. This saves time since it eliminates stripping it off the reel. Also, have at least 15–20 feet of line extending from the tip of the rod. This will help get the fly going faster and help build up power, or "load" the rod more quickly.

Keep in mind, too, that the longer the distance the rod covers between the back cast and forward cast, the more the rod is able to contribute to the cast. As the rod is raised it eliminates slack, starts the line moving faster and builds up power in the rod quickly, allowing you to get off a faster cast. If you start your back cast with the rod held too high, as many casters do, the rod will travel several feet before the line even moves, thus wasting valuable time getting the line going and building power in the rod. Start your back cast with the tip of your rod no more than a foot off the water, continuing as far back as you can for existing conditions, and then come forward with the forward cast, making sure to bring the rod parallel to the water. You will find this will greatly decrease the amount of time it takes to get your fly to the fish, but also, if done correctly, it will increase your distance in a single stroke of the rod. In essence, you will be breaking the standard nine o'clock, one o'clock casting technique, which works fine for fresh water, but which just isn't effective on the salt.

Another thing to help achieve greater distance is this: strip off 20–30 feet of line past the rod tip, leaving plenty of extra line on the deck or in the shooting basket. Start your cast, again, a foot off the water, lifting the rod with a quick upward motion, continuing into your back cast making sure to hold onto the line with your free hand. When you feel that the line has reached the end of the back cast, start your forward stroke, but just as the rod gets to a point even with your ear, pull downward on the line, releasing just before the rod becomes parallel with the water. This downward pull on the line, working with the power in the rod, will increase its forward speed and thus allow the line to travel further.

It is imperative to make sure there is ample excess line on the deck or in the shooting basket. If not, the line will shoot out only to come to a sudden stop without accomplishing your objective. Make sure the line is free, so that it will not snag on anything. It is also important not to commit too much downward pull on the line during the forward stroke. If you do, the sudden increase in speed may cause the line to loop over itself or the line and leader to loop together. Make the motion a steady pull, keeping in mind that you are only increasing line speed enough to obtain 20–30 more feet, not rocketing it across the bay. It may take some practice to get the right touch, but you will find this maneuver will help you achieve greater casting distances rather easily, especially in windy conditions.

CASTING TO HIT THE MARK

There are a couple of simple things to remember to achieve accuracy. The first is always to keep your eye on the target. When you see a fish, you should automatically know everything is ready and get a cast off without taking your eyes off the mark. Most saltwater species will show themselves only for a few seconds. In that short time, the angler should note in which direction the fish is traveling, hopefully getting the fly to him or in front of him before he goes down. If you take your eyes away to concentrate on the cast, the chance for success will be lost.

I like to compare casting accuracy with pitching a baseball or throwing a football. Eye contact (keeping your eye on the catcher's mitt or on the receiver throughout the motion), along with concentration, is everything. The same is true with casting a fly. The most accurate casters are those who can go through the motions of casting without taking their eyes or concentration off the target.

Another thing that will greatly increase your accuracy is to remember that where your fly goes is totally determined by the direction in which the rod tip stops at the end of the forward cast. That may sound like an obvious statement, but you'd be surprised at how many fly casters fail to hit their mark or are not able to make consistently accurate casts simply because they do not fully understand this principle.

Keeping the rod tip low to the water and removing the slack in the line prior to the back cast will help you get the fly to the target more accurately. However, it is important to get a straight back cast, which is done by stopping the rod on the back cast in the direction you want the fly to go. This is where many casters go wrong, simply because they have a bad habit of breaking their wrists. What happens when you break your wrist is this: when you reach the end of the back cast, the butt of the rod stops but the tip continues in motion, causing a dip in the line. Then, when you start your forward cast, the line is whipped around and thrown off course, missing the target.

The entire problem can easily be eliminated by keeping the wrist stiff throughout the cast. Think of your arm and rod as a single component. Start off with the rod tip low to the water with as little slack in the line as possible. Bring the rod up smoothly, quickly clearing the water, keeping the wrist stiff all through the back cast and until the final moment of the forward cast. Keep your eyes and concentration on the fish, and bring the rod parallel to the water. If you do this, you will find you will be much more accurate in your presentations.

You will notice, I say to keep the wrist stiff all through the back cast and **until the final moment of the forward cast,** or just prior to release of the line. The reason I say this is simple. In windy conditions it is easier to throw a line with a tight loop than a line with a big loop. A tighter loop also helps us achieve greater distance.

Loop size is controlled by wrist action. If you keep your wrist locked up to the point where the line is released you will develop a large, open loop which is what we do not want in most cases. So, to get a tighter loop, just before releasing the line, break the wrist with a quick, short forward motion. This will reduce the size of the loop in the line, cutting down on wind resistance, allowing for smoother, more accurate, and longer casts. This, also, requires some practice, but once you get the hang of it, you will quickly see its advantages.

FLY FISHING TACTICS

LOCATING THE GAME FISH

There are, of course, a number of different ways to fish for saltwater adversaries, and which is used really depends upon where you are fishing, at what depth the fish are holding or traveling, and wind and weather conditions. For example, trolling, blind-casting, chumming, and spot-casting are all productive, but only at specific times and under certain conditions. And in order to be successful, the angler must know which tactic is best at the time he is fishing. Let's take a look at each of these tactics.

Experience has taught me that blind-casting is the least productive method of fly fishing the salt. Because most tidal rivers, bays, and the ocean are so big, and fish are constantly on the move, the chances of hooking into a fish simply by casting a fly into the water are slight. It does happen, but often because the fly fisherman was lucky in his choice of spots, and the fish just happened to be there.

This does not mean blind-casting will not work. It will. However, it helps to know the likes and dislikes of the fish you are after, and it is a big help if you know an area well. Working an area on a certain tide can help, too. I know a particular spot of the Saco River in Maine where striped bass hold on the outgoing tide because the water is deep and baitfish are forced through the area as the tide recedes. This is a prime blind-casting area, but it took me several years to find it and know when it is most productive.

Trolling can be a productive tactic at times, especially when fishing large tidal rivers, bays, and offshore, when there's a chance fish are close to the surface, because it affords an opportunity to cover a lot of ground. I have caught many mackerel and bluefish while trolling, using a full-sinking fly line, short leaders, and a depth finder. The key is to find a school of fish, and, once it is found, to get the fly to the right depth and to stay with the school as it travels. Trolling a fly along jetties, breakwaters, in the mouths of rivers, along deep-cut banks, and along the shore just outside the surf is often productive, since these are all areas where baitfish are found.

In my mind, spot-fishing is one of the most productive and most exciting methods of fly fishing the salt, especially in rivers, shallow bays, and when the ocean is calm. You can spot-fish while a boat is anchored or moving, while wading, or from a pier or jetty, providing the fish is within casting range.

The key, of course, is being able to spot the fish prior to the cast, and, if working from a boat or wading, getting into position without forcing the fish down. Both require skill, which comes with time and trial and error. Knowing what to look for is also important, and there are several signs which can be extremely helpful.

Just about every saltwater fisherman knows that seagulls hovering overhead suggest fish below. This is often true, but it does not necessarily mean predator fish are there, only baitfish. It is the *action* of these birds which really tells you what is going on. If the gulls are circling, chances are no big game is around; the birds are simply watching and waiting for the carnage to begin. On the other hand, if the birds are dropping down in quick darts, apparently picking up bits of debris, it means the baitfish are being chased by something bigger, and that's the time to move in. A pair of field glasses will allow you to get a closer look at what exactly is going on.

Another well-known indicator that big fish are in the area is when you see baitfish breaking the surface, actually jumping clear of the water at times. They do this because striped bass, bluefish, or some other predator has moved in and, in a frenzy to escape, the smaller fish literally propel themselves into the air. I have seen this many times. On calm days, or even with a slight chop, the action can be spotted with the naked eye—but again, a pair of field glasses is a big aid, especially when covering a large bay.

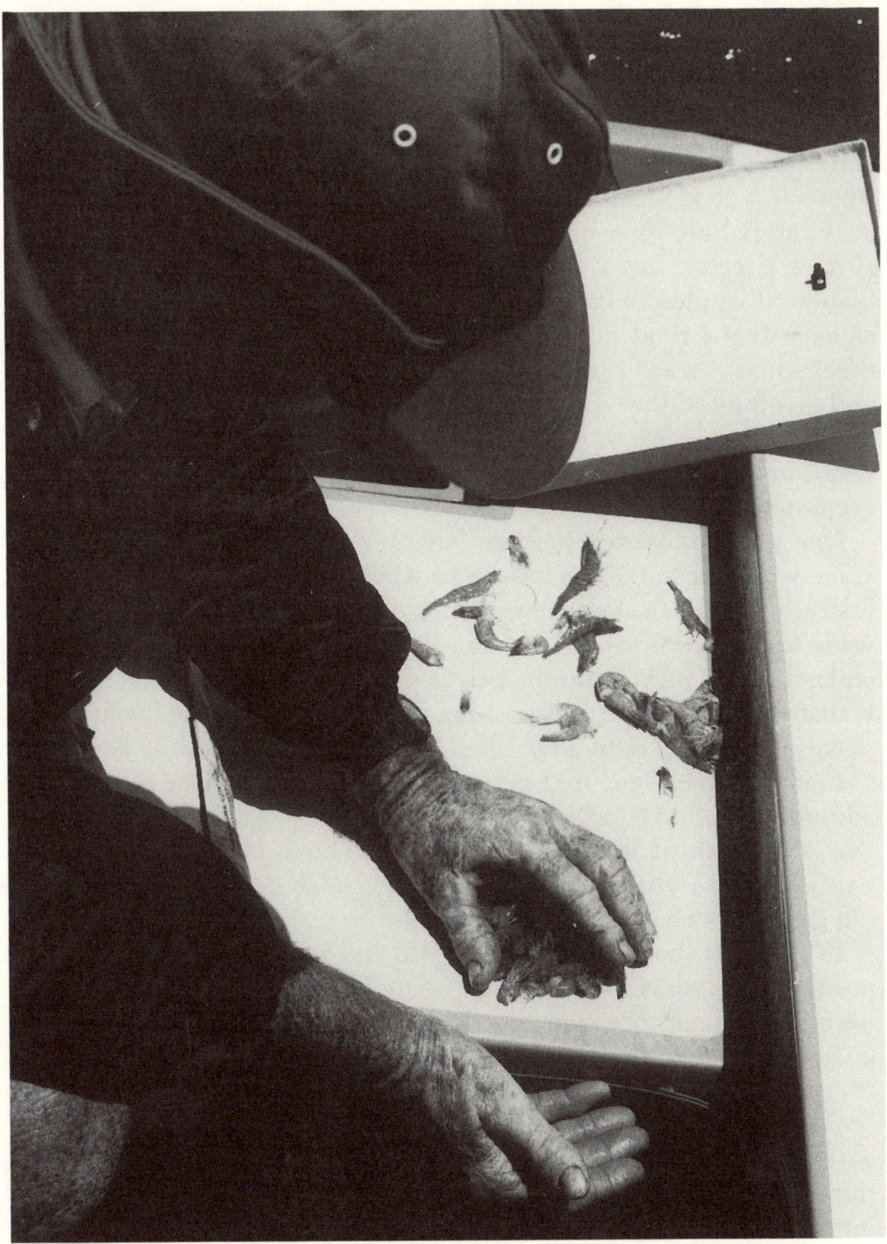

Chumming with shrimp. (Raychard photo)

Discolored water indicates baitfish, too. If you happen to notice an area where the water appears brownish or dark green, chances are it is a school of small fish. In this situation, it is often best to sit and wait and see what happens, or to approach the school slowly and make a series of casts into its middle, working the fly towards its outer edges. There is a good chance some larger game will be lurking nearby.

When fishing river mouths, bays, and even the open sea when the surface is calm, many saltwater fish will be found near the surface, giving off ripples as they cruise around. You can often pick up these signs without field glasses—but again, glasses will help. In either case, when you see this, check it out, making sure to approach slowly and carefully. Other signs you might see are boils and swirls. This is often true near piers, jetties, breakwaters, especially on the downwind, or calm, side. Whenever you see a boil or swirl, make a quick, accurate cast in that direction.

One problem spot-fishermen have is detecting baitfish and larger game when the surface is broken or when there are rolling waves and a steady wind. To overcome this dilemma, maneuver your boat or wade to a position where you can look directly into the wind, which will aid you in picking up the fish as they splash about. What happens is that the wind picks up the spray and pushes it towards you, which makes it easier to detect fish than when it is blowing away from you.

Finally, other signs that saltwater fishermen often see are seagulls and other sea birds floating in a bunch on the water. When you see this, stop the boat and sit. Chances are the birds picked up a school of baitfish while flying overhead and have settled down to wait until the big game moves in and starts feeding.

In either of these cases, getting your boat or wading into the right position is imperative to success. I hate to think of how many times I have seen a boat race over to a flock of gulls feeding in a certain area and the occupants start casting. The anglers knew that the birds suggested fish in the area, but their approach was all wrong.

Whenever you think a school of game fish is in an area, approach with care. Slow down and move in quietly, and never go racing into the middle of the frenzy. Stay at the outer edges, making your casts into the middle. This is where your long distance casting, accuracy, and ability to cast into the wind will come in handy.

The other productive form of saltwater fishing is chumming. What the angler does here is select a likely-looking spot and, either anchoring the boat or drifting, take some pre-cut bait, either crab, shrimp, clams, or baitfish, and simply toss it overboard for the purpose of attracting game fish. This tactic works quite well on mackerel, bluefish, striped bass, bonito, and shark off the Atlantic coast, and can be deadly once the angler learns what type of chum is best for a particular species and where game fish are apt to be located or traveling.

Which brings me to a final point: even if the angler is able to make long, accurate casts into the wind, it does little good unless he knows where the fish are. Like all good freshwater fishermen, saltwater anglers should get to know their adversaries well. Their likes and dislikes as far as food, habitat, and water conditions should be familiar. Know where these fish are apt to station themselves on various tides, and, in general, learn everything you possibly can about them. Many fishermen, for example, feel it is impossible to fish the surf with a fly rod. It can be difficult, especially from the beach, but with a boat working the surf is easy and highly productive. All kinds of saltwater fish, bluefish, mackerel, striped bass, even bonito will be found just off shore traveling up and down the beach in an attempt to escape larger predators. It also helps to know the depth of the water you are fishing and the depth different fish prefer.

Mackerel may be found in the shallows where there is less than 6 feet of water. Bluefish have been found in as little as 10 feet of water, as have bonito, while striped bass are apt to roam wherever there's food, especially at night. Keep in mind that all these fish, and most other saltwater species, will be found at deeper depths when they're forced there or when food is not available at shallower depths. On the other hand, if water temperatures are right and there is sufficient forage, shallow areas can produce dynamite action!

WADING AND NIGHT FISHING

Two tactics I would like to mention are wading and fishing at night. Both are highly productive, especially night fishing for striped bass, which has grown in popularity here in New England. Striped bass frequent tidal rivers, bays, and estuaries on nocturnal feeding runs, at which time they are extremely vulnerable to a well-placed streamer or popper. As a matter of fact, I have had some of my best bass fishing once the sun goes down. Along jetties, cut banks, piers, docks, and breakwaters are all prime nighttime areas. Lighted areas, such as marinas, are good, too. Keep in mind that fly size is extremely important with striped bass and, in the event of repeated refusals, a change in fly size rather than pattern will often make a difference. Pre-dawn fishing is productive, too, especially in late July and August when inshore water temperatures are warmest and striped bass are more willing to come in close.

Night fishing, like wading, should be done with EXTREME CAUTION. This is particularly true if the angler is unfamiliar with the terrain; it is essential to be aware of drop-offs, pot-holes, soft mud areas where it is possible to sink, and other hazards. In almost all cases, I prefer to explore during the day an area I plan on fishing at night. This allows me an opportunity to acquaint myself with any hidden secrets which might otherwise surprise me later.

Keep in mind, too, that your wading pace should be slow. When working along the banks of a tidal river or bay or even in the surf, I have found it a good idea to test the bottom in front of me before planting my foot. I also make a habit of dragging the toe of each foot which allows me to keep contact with the bottom so I know where it is at all times, and before putting the forward foot down I touch the bottom several times to make sure it is solid.

To prevent accident or injury while wading, always wear some foot protection. When fishing a sandy bottom I like sneakers, but sneakers are slippery on grass and rocks. A pair of wading boots with either felt soles or metal cleats is good, too. You might also find a wading staff handy, particularly for night fishing. It helps maintain balance and helps test the bottom in front of you. If you are wading and get caught in a tide, the best thing to do is turn sideways, allowing your body to cut into the current like the bow of a boat, and gradually work your way back. The main thing is not to panic and to take things slowly.

THE RETRIEVE

One thing many saltwater fly fishermen seem to overlook is the importance of the retrieve. Most saltwater species prefer a fast retrieve, but there are times when it is necessary to work the fly slowly or extremely fast. Keep in mind, however, that ocean dwellers, except for bottom fish, are fast swimmers and are accustomed to making quick or fast spurts when seeking baitfish. The slow retrieve just doesn't do the job. In fact, a fly being worked in the typical "freshwater style" will often be neglected, except perhaps when chumming in deep water when saltwater fish are being held in a certain area. Even then, when they strike, it is with a sudden acceleration in speed.

When you see a fish, for example, make your cast in front of him. Start your retrieve, and just before the fish gets to the fly, start stripping in fast. This will give the appearance of a frightened baitfish and will often entice the predator to strike. Slowing the retrieve or stopping altogether will usually make the fish lose interest completely—except, again, when chumming.

When blind-casting, it is often difficult to ascertain what speed of retrieve is right. This will be determined based upon water conditions, water depths, and what species you are after. However, here again, a fly traveling faster is more apt to entice a strike than one traveling slowly. When using chum, a slow retrieve will work, since the predator is feeding on dead fish; then, and only then, should the fly be worked slowly.

Fly fishermen often have problems with poppers. Poppers can be worked fast or slow, depending upon the fish and how that fish is feeding, but rarely is a saltwater popper worked as slowly as one used for freshwater bass. The important thing with poppers is to work them with a steady action and force them to make a disturbance on the surface. This can be done each time you make a pull on the line, or it can be done by sweeping the rod tip off to the side as you make your pull, making sure to keep slack to a minimum. This will speed up the retrieve, while giving the popper more action at the same time.

To get a really fast retrieve quite easily, which is often necessary, try this: after making a long cast, place your rod under your arm, and then bring in the line in a hand-over-hand retrieve. This is a dandy way of increasing your speed on long distance casts.

There is one other thing you should keep in mind when it comes to the speed of your retrieve. If a fish repeatedly misses the fly or passes it by, vary your speed, going faster first. Only after several different speeds should you try a different tactic, changing to a smaller or larger fly next, and a different pattern as a last resort.

THE STRIKE

I think one aspect of saltwater fly fishing which takes many enthusiasts by surprise is when a fish accepts their offering. Freshwater fly fishermen are used to soft rises and perhaps a sudden explosion every now and then on a streamer or bucktail.

Most saltwater species and most anadromous fish for that matter, react quite differently. They hit like a Mack truck in a surge of power and, unlike freshwater counterparts, they seem to go crazy once the hook is driven home. This often takes us by surprise and it is at this moment when many fish are lost.

The main objective once you think a fish has taken the fly is to set the hook. On saltwater fish, which have rather tough mouths, it is important to set the hook deep. This can be done in several ways, depending upon the size of the fish. The best way, in almost every situation, is to let the fish hook himself.

With some of the smaller saltwater fish like mackerel and many of the anadromous species (including sea-run trout, Atlantic salmon, coho salmon, and, to a lesser extent, shad) setting the hook is best done by simply lifting the rod. This motion expels all slack in the line and the downward action of the fish sets the hook. The trouble with shad is they have an extremely delicate mouth. Even so, it is imperative to set the hook deep hoping to get the hook into the roof of the mouth. The best way to do this is to give a sudden upward jerk on the rod making sure the line is taut. You'll either set the hook solidly or lose the fish, at that point, which is what will happen anyway unless you get the hook deep.

When it comes to hooking the larger saltwater fish, however, more than lifting the rod is often needed to drive the hook home. Two ways I have tried are simple and work quite well.

When a fish strikes, keeping your rod tip low to the water and pointed in the direction of the fish, simply grasp the line and pull straight back towards you. This sets the hook deep and fast since the hook is being pulled in one direction as the fish travels in another. It is important, however, to make sure your access line is free on the deck or in the shooting basket, and that you immediately release the line after setting the hook. The fish will often make a powerful, distant run at this point, and keeping pressure on the line with your hand will only result in a break-off. Allow him to run with the fly.

Another tactic is somewhat unorthodox, but it works. When the fish strikes, lower the rod tip and move it to right angles to the boat or fish, making sure to hold onto the line with your free hand. As the fish moves away he actually hooks himself. Once you feel the hook has been set, release the line immediately.

Your next problem is to make sure the line lying on the deck or in the shooting basket goes off smoothly. If it gets tangled around an anchor or oar handle, forget it—the fish is lost.

To prevent this, once the fish is solidly hooked, forget about the fish. The hook is where it should be and will not dislodge. Concentrate on the line until all of it has been cleared. In many cases it helps to hold the line high at this point, giving you time and space to untangle any loops.

Playing and landing saltwater and anadromous fish have challenges, too, and unless the fly fisherman knows how to handle the situation, and take command, the battle will be lost. By following a few basic rules and keeping certain things in mind, however, even the inexperienced angler can do quite well.

The key to winning the battle with any big game fish, no matter where it is found, is never to allow a sharp jerk against the line. The leader will split or the hook will dislodge. If you keep a steady pull on the fish, the line will last. To reduce the shock of a sudden surge, the fisherman should thrust his rod towards the fish the moment the run begins, rather than pull the rod towards himself. If you pull the rod

(Raychard photo)

towards you, you are increasing the tension and jerking impact on the line, which causes something to give, most often, the leader or the flesh.

It is also important to get the fish under control and take command of the situation as soon after the fly has been hit as possible, keeping in mind that the further away from you a fish travels, the more difficult it is to get him back. During the first moments of the initial run, the angler can slow the fish down by keeping steady pressure on the line, but there is little he can do to stop him. Don't try to overpower the fish at this point—let him run, keeping the line at a steady pressure.

Once the fish has stopped—then, take command. At all times either the angler or the fish should be taking line, with no periods when the line is dead or slack. Keep your rod tip up when reeling in, lowering the tip quickly if there is a sudden surge. If you get to a point where the fish cannot be budged, try pumping the rod several times, remembering to reel in line only when the rod is being lowered, never on the upswing. This would only increase tension.

When a fish jumps, as saltwater and anadromous species often do, it is again important to take tension off the line. This is best done by quickly lowering the rod tip to the surface of the water. This reduces the chances of splitting the leader, and of the fish rolling into the leader and pulling the fly from its mouth.

Our problems arise when the fish finally gets close to the boat or net. You can often shorten the battle by providing some side pressure to the fish. When the fish gets in close, take your rod and hold it at right angles to the direction the fish is swimming. This forces the fish onto its side and throws him off balance while using up his energy, all of which aids the angler.

LANDING THE BIG ONES

Landing a big saltwater or anadromous fish is always an adventure. So much can go wrong, and so quickly, that even experienced fishermen are learning new ways to do it better. Certain things can make landing a fish easier. No fish should be netted or gaffed if you plan to release it, however, and this is true of bluefish and striped bass as well as Atlantic salmon and shad. If you plan to release the fish, keep it in the water and, using a pair of long-nose pliers, dislodge the hook or cut the leader.

But if you do plan to net the fish, make sure your net is big enough to handle it. Nets with handles that extend are extremely helpful and overall, are the best. Be aware that chasing the fish with a net is a "no-no". Place the net in the water and lead the fish to it head first, never from the rear. A sudden touch of the tail can send the fish into a surge which will most likely break the leader.

Gaffing a fish, like a bluefish, requires cooperation and timing between the fisherman and the person doing the actual gaffing. The two should communicate with one another, the fisherman telling the partner when to gaff. The person with the gaff should wait for the word, and when he gets it, make sure never to lunge or stab at the fish. He should lower the gaff into the water slowly, working it into position, and then work upward with a single, quick motion, making sure he stays in back of the leader. That way if the fish makes a sudden drive, the gaff will not come in contact with the leader. Also, once the fish has been gaffed and is lifted out of the water, the fisherman should lower his rod immediately, taking tension off the line.

All fish react differently when netted or gaffed. Caution should be taken at all times, especially with such species as bluefish and shark, which are difficult to kill and have sharp teeth. While most anglers can handle a bluefish, and remove a fly by wearing a pair of gloves and covering the eyes with forefinger and thumb and squeezing, thus immobilizing the fish, sharks, for example, should never be boated. The best way to kill a shark is by towing it behind the boat.

Always respect these fish when handling them. Almost all saltwater species have something sharp somewhere on their bodies—teeth, gill covers, or fins— which can cut or cause other injury.

TACTICS FOR THE ANADROMOUS SPECIES

Finding, casting to, hooking, playing, and landing the anadromous species require a mixture of freshwater and saltwater tactics. Once these fish have entered a river, they hold to many of the same areas that brook trout and landlocked salmon do, which are primarily deep, cool, well-oxygenated pools and riffles. Hooking these fish, with an uplifting of the rod, playing them once hooked, and landing them demand the same respect as saltwater species, largely due to their size, stamina and great power. In many ways, the anadromous fish draws out the best in the fly fisherman, for he must be acquainted with, and have skills for both worlds in order to be successful.

Each of the fish found along the New England coast and in our rivers is unique, and for that reason, it might be best to cover each one individually to obtain a better understanding of its character and how best to fish for it.

The Atlantic Salmon is without question the best known and most illustrious anadromous game fish in New England. Today they are found in fishable numbers in several Maine rivers (see Chapter 6); attempts are also being made to reintroduce the sea-run salmon to several ancestral rivers in southern New England.

From an angling perspective the Atlantic salmon is a superior game fish. They are a challenge to fish over and, once hooked, provide an exhilarating battle few other fish can match. It is widely known that enticing these warriors to the fly is rarely easy. However, understanding the salmon, knowing their likes and dislikes for water habitat and holding areas, when they will be found in a river, what draws them upstream, and what tactics to use makes things easier. It will not guarantee success, but it will help.

Generally, Atlantic salmon enter a home river during the spring, most often in May and June on a rise of water from spring run-off, a period of rain, or high tide. On some rivers there is also a fall run, but in Maine the largest number of fish will be found moving upstream and actually in the river in the spring.

The best scenario for the Atlantic salmon is when rivers are running moderately high but relatively clear. Heavy, discolored water makes for poor action while at the other extreme, low, clear water that has had a chance to warm takes away all sense of cooperation. These fish are fussy and will not accept a fly if water conditions and flow are not right. They can be highly cooperative one day, and nowhere to be found the next, if a sudden rain storm increases water flow or taints the river.

When holding in a river, Atlantic salmon will select spots above or below areas that require energy to pass through and navigate, since they utilize water flow to guide themselves upstream to their spawning grounds. They are seldom (if ever) found in dead water areas, preferring a steady flow anywhere in the mainstream in depths ranging from several feet to several inches. Anglers familiar with salmon look for points, rocks, boulders, ledges—anything that breaks the current in which a resting spot is available. The tail end of pools and the head of pools are other potential areas, providing that the salmon has something to hide behind, that there is a steady flow, and that there is easy access to the mainstream.

(Diane Dery photo)

Just about all fly fishing for Atlantic salmon in Maine is done with sub-surface flies, streamers, and bucktails that range from the basic to the complicated. They work best in the spring when water levels are high and temperatures are low. The most productive patterns are tied on hooks ranging from size 4 to 8 for normal flow conditions, while larger sizes such as 3/0 and 2 are often used in high, discolored conditions. In time and with experience, the salmon fisherman will develop a good idea as to what size fly to use first, based upon water conditions. But because these fish are touchy, it is always a good idea to have a number of patterns in varied sizes. As mentioned in Chapter 3, patterns such as the Cosseboom, Black Bear Hair flies with green, orange and yellow butts, the Coburn Special, Durham Ranger, Rusty Rat, Silver Rat, Blue Charm, Muddler, and Green Highlander are all popular. There are, however, many other designs that will produce results, and it is always best to check with a local fly shop for any local favorites, especially if you are unfamiliar with the river in question.

One of the biggest problems a novice Atlantic salmon fisherman has to overcome is the instinct to try setting the hook when he sees a fish rise to the fly. Unlike trout and freshwater fishing, where the angler must set the hook, it is imperative to resist lifting the rod when a salmon rises. When a fish comes up to the fly, hold the rod motionless until you actually feel the fish, and then lift the rod tip and reel in the slack. The salmon will hook himself. If the salmon jumps, which he most likely will, remember to lower the rod tip, giving him his head and releasing tension. If he gets into a position where you cannot move him, you can do one of two things: you can try pumping him, remembering to reel in line only when the rod is on the downward swing, or you can lower the rod to the water surface and give him line. What this does is give the salmon the idea that he is free, at which time he will generally move on his own. Be prepared when you add pressure, however, for he will usually repeat his initial run with a surge of power broken by a series of leaps during which the rod tip should be lowered each time.

Casting to Atlantic salmon is not too difficult, and is often in an across and slightly downstream fashion. The idea is to cover as much water as you can; because salmon are often stationed only a few feet from shore, start off with a short cast and gradually work outward. Once you have reached the maximum distance you can cast, move downstream several feet and start again.

Theoretically, your fly should travel at such a speed that it allows the salmon to see it, but not so fast that it passes his station in a flash. It takes time and practice to develop the right speed, but it helps if you cast directly across stream in slow water, and slightly downstream in faster areas, mending the line upstream to slow it down, mending downstream to speed it up, if necessary.

It also helps to cast your fly in such a way that it drifts broadside to the fish, giving him a clear view of it. This can be done by utilizing the greased line method. This is done by casting across and quartering downstream, mending line upstream every time there is slack or the line bellies. You should follow the fly with your rod tip, keeping the line as straight as possible. This method is often used in conjunction with a riffle hitch, which helps keep the fly at a right angle to the current and which helps the fly skim across the surface or just below the surface, depending upon the speed of drift. In many cases, this technique will draw a response when everything else fails.

Some of the best Atlantic salmon fishing in Maine is found early in the morning, from sunrise to about 9 A.M.,and then again in the late afternoon to dusk, especially when the day breaks bright and clear. On overcast days, salmon may remain active longer and may even be enticed to a fly when the sun is high. Generally, however, it is best to concentrate your efforts early or late in the day.

During the peak salmon weeks, the fly fisherman should use a floating line, in a weight-forward taper. During the extreme early season when water flows are high, a sinking-tip line might come in handy, but just about every fisherman you see on Maine rivers will be using a floater once water flows reach normal flow. Leaders should be 7 to 9 feet in length and in the 8–10 pound test class. Level mono leaders are fine, although there are some who insist tapered leaders are better.

Presently 11 Maine rivers offer Atlantic salmon fishing opportunities. All fishing in freshwater portions is restricted to fly fishing only, and specific rules and regulations govern each. A special salmon license is required. Those rivers which have salmon include the Penobscot, Aroostook, St. Croix, Saco, Union, Machias, East Machias, Narraguagus, Pleasant, Sheepscot, and Dennys. The Penobscot, Narraguagus, Dennys, and St. Croix are usually the top producers.

COHO SALMON. Fly fishing for coho salmon, which are now found in several New England rivers (in New Hampshire and Massachusetts) is a somewhat different game. You can use a floating line for these fish when found in shallow riffles and pools, but on most occasions a floating/sink-tip line is best. These fish hug the bottom much of the time and, while they will come up for a fly, your best chances for action will come when you get the fly down to the fish and right under his nose. Also, the best fishing comes in the fall, in September and October, although activity may continue well into December.

The best fly rod for coho salmon is one of about 9 feet in length designed for a 7- or 8-weight line, just like for Atlantic salmon. Make sure your reel has ample backing; these fish do not jump like an Atlantic, but in the current have sufficient power to rip off considerable lengths of line. Your leaders should be in the 10–12 pound test range, considering the size of these fish and their bull-like characteristics and habit of rolling over into the leader.

One big problem many fly fishermen have with the coho salmon is getting a good solid set of the hook due to the weird shape of its mouth, which is open on the sides, especially in the males. I have missed many simply because I failed to get the barb into the top of the mouth or jaw. It is something that happens to everyone, and the best way to increase your chances is to wait to lift the rod until you feel the fish. At that point, lift the rod tip with a solid jerk and pray you hit meat.

In general, I feel New England's coho fishery is an exciting one. It offers a chance to wet a line and catch some impressive fish when things are slowing down for the year, but, unfortunately, the runs are highly unpredictable and at times, very spotty. Also, coho are found in only a few rivers: the Lamprey River in New Hampshire and the North River area of Massachusetts. I feel that the interest among New England fly fishermen is not as high as it could be, although, during years when the runs are high and word gets out, there is a fair amount of pressure. In any event, it is certainly worth the effort to cast a fly for these West Coast transplants. A list of productive flies will be found in Chapter 3, while more detailed information on both of the rivers they inhabit will be found in Chapter 6.

SHAD is a fairly abundant fish in New England and at certain points south to Chesapeake Bay, yet it remains somewhat under-utilized by the fly fishing fraternity. I think it important and beneficial to cover, if only briefly, some basic tactics needed to catch this wonderful gamefish. (See Chapters 2 and 3 for more specific information about flies and tackle and for a discussion of sea-run brown trout).

The important thing to remember about shad is, when found in fresh water, they prefer moving current, riffles, and the edges of the mainstream, just like Atlantic salmon; they are almost always found hugging the bottom. However, unlike the salmon, they will seldom come up to a fly, so it is necessary to go down after them. Obviously, you will require flies that sink well and a high-density full sinking fly line. Don't worry about making long casts. In most situations, especially when fishing from a boat, it is only necessary to cast 30 feet or so, and then allow the fly to sink to the bottom. It is then allowed to

VALENTINE
MADE IN USA

mend into the current and worked upstream in a series of quick, short spurts covering 12–14 inches on each pull. If no response comes, you can either make another cast or simply allow the current to take the fly back downstream by letting out excess line.

It is also important to remember that the shad has a soft, fragile mouth, so playing these fish gently is a key to success. Flies tied on hook sizes 4, 6, and 8 are generally preferred with the larger sizes used most often in fast water, the smaller sizes in slow, clear water. Water temperature apparently plays a major role in shad activity. The most desirable water temperatures appear to be between 55 and 63 degrees, which is when shad actually spawn and therefore are most active.

Opposite: These "Shad Bumps" are fluorescent orange, pink, red, and green chenille wrapped "babine" style on weighted gold-plated hooks to help them sink. The chenille is covered with lacquer for durability. An extremely easy and inexpensive fly to tie, it is deadly on shad. (Diane Dery photo)

Chapter 6

WHERE TO GO AND WHO TO CONTACT: *New England*

With a coastline several thousand miles long and hundreds of rivers and streams where saltwater and anadromous fish will be found during the spring and fall, it would appear that the fly fisherman here in New England has it easy when it comes to finding water in which to wet a fly.

There is no doubt we have plenty of areas and water to choose from—so many, in fact, we might be overpowered by it all unless we keep it in proper perspective. Above all else, the saltwater fly fisherman should keep in mind that casting a fly for blues or striped bass is, in many ways, like casting a fly to brook trout or landlocked salmon. Once you know where to look and can handle various demands and situations, it all becomes relative and falls into place.

When I first started fly fishing salt water a number of years ago, I found myself in the same predicament as many first-time fly fishermen. I live within a few minutes' drive of the sea and only a short walk from a tidal river, but still, the question, "Where do I go?" persisted. Finally, the urge to try casting a fly in the salt got the best of me. I took the initiative, and that was the first major step. I picked up my fly rod and vest, walked down to the river and went at it. I knew little about what to do, but I put my freshwater experience to use, and, if memory serves me correctly, I had little success. I did manage to entice a couple of small tinker mackerel to the fly (which increased my encouragement and faith), but it wasn't until I caught my first bluefish a year later, and then my first striped bass, that I became totally hooked. As my desire to pursue saltwater fly fishing grew, that old question, "Where do I go?" kept coming back.

I quickly discovered, however, that fly fishing in a bay or river where anadromous species are found is no different than fly fishing a trout pond or freshwater stream. Once you spend time getting to know the different species and a certain area, experience tells you when the fishing is apt to be most productive.

So it is on the sea. All saltwater fish will be found inshore, in a bay or river, at certain times of the year, based upon water temperature, food, weather conditions, the time of year, and tides. The same is true, for the most part, with anadromous species. The first step in answering "Where do I go?" is to learn as much about the various species as possible. We have tried to break the ice in the previous chapters, but much more will come with time and on-water experience. Once you learn what the various fish like, and don't like, you will have a good idea where and when they are most likely to be available.

As for finding specific areas to fish, I think the novice fly fisherman has more trouble than the more experienced angler simply because the man who has been at it for a few years has already explored several areas and knows when those spots are active.

There are several good ways for the novice saltwater fly fisherman to find productive water. The first is to find a fellow fly fisherman who is more experienced and develop a friendship. I have found this extremely easy to do, since saltwater fly fishermen are a minority among the saline anglers, and most are looking for companionship and someone to share their time and experience with. Good places to start looking are at local fish and game clubs, fishing groups, and the like. Attend one of their meetings and chances are good that you will bump into someone who is into fly fishing the salt.

Another good way is simply to talk to saltwater fishermen in general. They know when bluefish are apt to be in a certain river or when stripers move into a particular bay, even what tides and times of day are traditionally best. This is all data the fly fisherman can use and rely on, and simply asking questions and developing a rapport with another angler is one of the easiest and best ways to discover productive fishing areas. Again, your odds of bumping into a saltwater or anadromous enthusiast at a local fish and game club or fishing group meeting are excellent.

Another good source of information, as I have mentioned before, are local bait and tackle shops, of which there are many along the coast. Much of the time the owners and proprietors of these shops are more than willing to provide helpful information—even if you don't buy anything. It's only good business sense. Several years ago when I started traveling more and more to areas I had never been to before, I started keeping a little book of shop names and telephone numbers up and down the coast where information might be obtained. It is a good way to put your hands on up-to-the minute conditions, and I recommend that you do the same.

One of the best ways for the inexperienced fly fisherman to familiarize himself with a specific area is to hire the services of a reputable charter boat captain for a couple of days. A great many of these guys cater to anglers for a living. They know their business, they know the area they work in, and where the fish are at certain times of the season and on different tides, and they can aid the angler not only in finding fish, but can teach him something as well. The cost of a charter is well worth the investment, and a good captain's knowledge, advice, and expertise can prove invaluable. But charter boat services don't come cheap. Most cost $150–$250 per day. Here's what to do: round up two or three fishing buddies and go together, even if they don't fly fish. The cost in almost all cases is for the boat per day, not angler per day, which divided four ways makes things more affordable.

Of course, finding a charter service in a specific area, as well as a reliable source of information, such as a bait or tackle shop, can take time. And, as all fishermen will agree, time during the fishing season is valuable—to many, priceless. There are, however, a couple of things the angler can do to save time and money, allowing him to select where he wants to fish based upon sound information prior to the actual day out or trip. The key is to start planning early to get a jump on the season.

First, any New England fly fisherman serious about saltwater and/or anadromous species fishing should seriously consider subscribing to *The Fisherman* magazine, the New England Edition. This magazine has an annual subscription rate of $20.00 (as of 1989) but it is published weekly, except for two weeks in December, so you get 50 issues. Although *The Fisherman* publishes both fresh and saltwater articles, it is primarily oriented to the saltwater enthusiast, and contains many where-to-go type articles, covering specific areas.

More important, however, for the fisherman looking for a good source of contacts and charter services, are the magazine's ads. There are dozens of bait and tackle shops and charter services listed, from Maine to Connecticut and Rhode Island. I have used several, finding out about fishing action, tides, and everything else needed to plan a visit simply by picking up the phone and making a few calls or by writing a few letters of inquiry. It is important to check around early, particularly with charter services, since many are booked up well in advance, especially during prime fishing weeks.

Several other regional magazines are available, too, all of which address saltwater fishing, although not necessarily saltwater fly fishing. In Maine, there is *The Maine Sportsman* which has several coastal report writers and other contributors writing from time to time on saltwater fishing and fishing for anadromous fish. There is also *New England Out-of-Doors* magazine and *Northeast Woods & Waters* magazine, both of which are published in Massachusetts, but which cover all of New England, including the coast. Both have coastal columnists, and feature articles on saltwater fishing and fishing for shad, Atlantic salmon, and coho salmon on occasion, most stressing where-to-go formats. For additional information on these magazines write:

THE FISHERMAN
P.O. Box 211
2 Dennison Ave.
Mystic, CT 06355

NORTHEAST WOODS & WATERS
P.O. Box 38
Chicopee, MA 01014

THE MAINE SPORTSMAN
P.O. Box 507
Yarmouth, ME 04096

SALTWATER SPORTSMAN
184 Lincoln Street
Boston, MA 02111

NEW ENGLAND OUT-OF-DOORS
510 King Street
P.O. Box 248
Littleton, MA 01460

Fishermen can also contact respective state fish and wildlife or department of environmental conservation offices. All charter services and bait and tackle shops must be registered or licensed, and a letter or telephone call will usually get you a listing which can easily be put to use. When you contact these offices, ask for a listing of licensed charter boats and, if possible, a list of bait dealers. (It is doubtful a list of tackle shops will be available, but most fish and wildlife or DEC offices do license bait shops.)

Connecticut Dept. of Commerce
210 Washington Street
Hartford, CT 06106
Tel: (203) 722-3530
(For a list of charter boats)

Connecticut Dept. of Environmental Protection
State Office Bldg.
Hartford, CT 06115
Tel: (203) 566-5599

Maine Dept. of Fish & Wildlife
284 State Street
Augusta, ME 04333
Tel: (207) 289-2871

Maine Dept. of Marine Resources
Augusta, ME 04330
Tel: (207) 289-2291
(For a list of charter boats)

Massachusetts Div. of Fisheries & Wildlife
Leverett Saltonstall Bldg.
100 Cambridge Street
Boston, MA 02202
Tel: (617) 727-3151

Massachusetts Div. of Fisheries & Wildlife
RFD 3
Buzzards Bay, MA 02532
Tel: (508) 759-3406
(For the Cape Cod area)

New Hampshire Div. of Economic Development
Concord, NH 03301
Tel: (603) 271-1110

New Hampshire Fish & Game Dept.
34 Bridge Street
Concord, NH 03301
Tel: (800) 852-3411
(603) 271-3127

Rhode Island Dept. of Economic Development
One Weybosset Hill
Providence, RI 02903
Tel: (401) 277-2611
(For a list of charter boats)

Rhode Island Dept. of Natural Resources
Veterans Memorial Bldg.
Providence, RI 02903
Tel: (401) 227-2784

One quick and convenient way of getting up-to-the-minute fishing information on salmon and anadromous fishing conditions is by calling the **Salmon Unlimited Hotline.** When you call, you will get a recording asking for your name and telephone number. A representative will call back later, and will answer any question you might have on Atlantic salmon, coho salmon, and shad fishing in New England. The telephone number is (603) 627-9702. If you wish to join Salmon Unlimited, or would like further information, write them at P.O. Box 339, Greenland, NH 03840.

Getting started in any new endeavor is difficult, time-consuming and costly; this is also true of saltwater fly fishing. Many of us are cautious at first, wanting to test the waters, so to speak, before diving right in. This only makes good sense, which is why starting out on a tidal river or bay close to home makes even more sense. There is no sense in taking the time and driving to Cape Cod and chartering a boat for a day or two until you have some indication whether saltwater fishing is something you will enjoy. On the other hand, there is argument in favor of fishing a hotspot like Cape Cod and, indeed, chartering a boat right from the start. Doing so will get you started in the right direction, get you into some action from the beginning, while showing you the ropes, building interest and confidence. It is a fair and worthwhile argument, and something you might want to consider seriously.

In most cases, I think breaking the ice close to home is best, especially if you already fish the salt with lures and bait. Chances are you know the area, which is an important factor, and it doesn't cost a whole lot, which often governs whether we fish or not. Also, because the area is so close, you can fish it often, which only increases your experience and interest. After you have been at it awhile, or when fly fishing the salt is definitely something you want to pursue, then explore other areas, putting the knowledge and skills you have developed to use, for what you learn close to home will often work in unfamiliar waters as well.

On the following pages are listed some of the better fishing areas along the New England coast and some of the top rivers where anadromous species might be available. We will not attempt to cover these areas in great detail; we will leave the in-depth exploring and discovery to the individual fly fisherman. But we will suggest some areas where fishing is known to be cooperative, with the sincere hope that these suggestions will get you started in the right direction.

MAINE

Maine's ragged coastline stretches some 2,500 miles from Eastport to Kittery, and within that distance the fly fisherman will find some of the finest and most varied saltwater and anadromous angling in all of New England. The Maine offshore fishing season, as well as the angling in coastal rivers, traditionally starts later than areas to the south (due to the chill water conditions), with action starting in June, running through July, August, and into mid-September.

AREA	SPECIES AVAILABLE
WASHINGTON COUNTY:	
Cobscook Bay	Mackerel, Bluefish, occasional Striped bass
Dennys River	Atlantic salmon
East Machias River	Atlantic salmon, Shad
Jonesport, Beals Island	Mackerel, Bluefish, occasional Striped bass
Machias River	Atlantic salmon
Millbridge, Narraguagus Bay	Mackerel
Narraguagus River	Atlantic salmon, Shad
HANCOCK COUNTY:	
Bar Harbor/Mt. Desert Island	Mackerel, Pollock
Frenchman Bay	Mackerel, Bluefish, occasional Striped bass
Sorrento Harbor	Mackerel
Sullivan River/West Sullivan	Mackerel
Union River and Bay	Atlantic salmon, Mackerel
Blue Hill Harbor	Mackerel, Pollock
Bagaduce River/ South Penobscot	Mackerel, Striped bass

AREA	SPECIES AVAILABLE
WALDO COUNTY:	
Stockton Harbor	Mackerel, Striped bass
Searsport Harbor	Striped bass, Mackerel, Bluefish
Bayside/East Northport	Mackerel
Penobscot River and Bay	Striped bass, Bluefish, Mackerel
PENOBSCOT COUNTY:	
Penobscot River	Atlantic salmon, Striped bass, Shad
KNOX COUNTY:	
Weskeag River/So. Thomaston	Mackerel, Striped bass
Rockport Harbor	Mackerel, Bluefish, Striped bass
Seal Harbor/Sprucehead	Striped bass, Pollock, Bluefish
Port Clyde	Mackerel, Pollock
St. George River/Thomaston	Mackerel, Striped bass, occasional Bluefish
Meduncook River/East Friendship	Mackerel, Striped bass
Hatchet Cove/Friendship	Mackerel, Striped bass, Bluefish, Pollock
LINCOLN COUNTY:	
New Harbor	Pollock, Mackerel, Bluefish, Striped bass
Round Pond	Striped bass, Bluefish, Mackerel
Muscongus Harbor	Mackerel, Bluefish, Striped bass, Pollock
Medomak River	Mackerel, Bluefish, Striped bass
Boothbay Harbor	Mackerel, Bluefish, Striped bass, Pollock
Pemaquid River and Pemaquid Point	Mackerel, Pollock, Bluefish

AREA	SPECIES AVAILABLE
LINCOLN COUNTY (CONT'D.)	
Damariscotta River	Striped bass, Bluefish, Mackerel
Sheepscot River/Back River/ Hodgdon Island	Atlantic salmon, Mackerel, Striped bass
Sheepscot/Alna on Sheepscot River	Atlantic salmon
SAGADAHOC COUNTY:	
Reid State Park/Georgetown	Mackerel, Pollock, Striped bass, Bluefish
Kennebec River/Fort Popham	Striped bass, Bluefish, Mackerel, Pollock
Kennebec River/Phippsburg	Striped bass, Bluefish, Mackerel
Kennebec River/Bath	Striped bass, Bluefish, Mackerel
Cundy's Harbor/ New Meadows River	Mackerel, Bluefish, Striped bass
CUMBERLAND COUNTY:	
Basin Point/Potts Harbor	Mackerel
Royal River	Sea-run brown trout
Falmouth Foreside	Bluefish, Striped bass, Mackerel
Presumpscot River	Bluefish, Striped bass, Mackerel, Sea-run brown trout, occasional Coho salmon
Crescent Beach State Park	Mackerel, Bluefish, Striped bass
Pine Point	Mackerel, Bluefish, Striped bass

AREA	SPECIES AVAILABLE
YORK COUNTY:	
Saco River	Mackerel, Bluefish, Striped bass, Atlantic salmon, Coho salmon, Pollock
Wells/Webhannet River	Bluefish, Striped bass, Mackerel
Ogunquit River	Sea-run brown trout, Mackerel, Pollock, occasional Coho salmon
Pepperell Cove/Kittery	Mackerel, Bluefish, Striped bass, Pollock, Coho salmon

NEW HAMPSHIRE

Despite the fact that New Hampshire has the shortest coastline of any New England state, stretching barely 30 miles as the crow flies, some excellent and quality angling is possible in a number of spots. The saltwater action starts up in early June, peaking in July and August, with sporadic action into mid-September. At that time, river fishing for anadromous species such as coho salmon begins, continuing until early winter.

AREA	SPECIES AVAILABLE
STRAFFORD AND ROCKINGHAM COUNTIES:	
Little Bay/Great Bay/ Piscataqua River	Bluefish, Striped bass, Mackerel, Coho salmon
Wallis Sands/Rye North Beach/ Rye Beach/Little Boars Head	Bluefish, Striped bass, Mackerel, Pollock
Hampton Beach/Hampton Harbor/ Seabrook Beach	Striped bass, Bluefish, Mackerel

MASSACHUSETTS

Ask any hardened saltwater fisherman where he would like to spend the majority of his time, and chances are he will say Massachusetts—probably, Cape Cod. Without question the Commonwealth offers the finest saltwater fishing in New England, with the Cape being the center of attention. This is largely due to the fact that it sticks out into the Atlantic, and its warm water currents attract many species of fish.

Fishing along the Massachusetts coast begins in late May in areas north of Cape Cod, a couple weeks earlier at points south. Fishing on the south side of the Cape, in Buzzards Bay, Vineyard Sound, and around Martha's Vineyard, Nantucket, and Monomoy Island is often productive well into October, offering the fisherman a relatively long season.

From Salisbury (on the New Hampshire border) to the Rhode Island border (on the south), Massachusetts enjoys a coastline some 1,500 miles long, the second longest coastline in New England. Saltwater fishing is extremely popular, attracting large crowds on weekends during the spring, summer, and fall. Visiting enthusiasts, therefore, should not expect to have an area to themselves. There is, however, plenty of water and fish to go around; and there is even some fine sea-run brown trout and coho salmon fishing in the fall as well.

AREA	SPECIES AVAILABLE
ESSEX COUNTY:	
Salisbury/Newburyport/Plum Island	Bluefish, Striped bass, Mackerel, Pollock, occasional Bonito
Merrimack River	Shad, Striped bass, Bluefish, Mackerel

AREA	SPECIES AVAILABLE
ESSEX COUNTY (CONT'D.)	
Parker River	Sea-run brown trout, Bluefish, Striped bass, Mackerel
Ipswich River	Striped bass, Bluefish
PLYMOUTH COUNTY:	
North River	Sea-run brown trout, Coho salmon, Shad
Kingston Bay/Plymouth	Stripers, Bluefish, Mackerel, occasional Bonito, occasional Weakfish
Jones River/Kingston	Sea-run brown trout
Beaverdam Brook/Plymouth	Sea-run brown trout
Wareham/Rochester	Bluefish, Striped bass, Bonito, Shark, Weakfish, Albacore, Pollock, Mackerel
BARNSTABLE COUNTY:	
Cape Cod Canal	Striped bass, Weakfish, Bluefish
Scorton Creek/Sandwich	Sea-run brown trout
Barnstable/Santuit Creek	Sea-run brown trout, Bluefish, Striped bass, Mackerel
Brewster/East Brewster	Striped bass, Bluefish, Mackerel, Bonito, Shark
Wellfleet Harbor	Striped bass, Bluefish, Mackerel, Bonito, Albacore, Shark
Orleans/East Orleans	Striped bass, Bluefish, Mackerel, Bonito, Weakfish, Albacore
Monomoy Island	Striped bass, Bluefish, Bonito, Cobia
Sequetucket Harbor/ South Yarmouth	Striped bass, Bluefish, Bonito, Cobia

AREA	SPECIES AVAILABLE
BARNSTABLE COUNTY (CONT'D)	
Lewis Bay/Craigville Beach	Striped bass, Bluefish, Bonito, Pollock, Albacore, Cobia
Cotuit Bay	Striped bass, Bluefish, Bonito, Pollock, Mackerel, Weakfish, Cobia, Albacore, Shark
Mashpee River	Sea-run brown trout
Falmouth/Falmouth Heights	Bluefish, Striped bass, Bonito, Shark, Pollock, Albacore, Cobia, Mackerel
Coonamessett River/Child's River/ Quashnet River	Sea-run brown trout
Buzzards Bay	Bluefish, Striped bass, Bonito, Pollock, Mackerel, Weakfish, Cobia, Albacore, Shark
NANTUCKET COUNTY:	
Nantucket Sound/Nantucket Island	Bluefish, Striped bass, Bonito, Pollock, Mackerel, Weakfish, Albacore, Shark
DUKES COUNTY:	
Martha's Vineyard	Bluefish, Striped bass, Bonito, Pollock, Mackerel, Weakfish, Albacore, Shark
BRISTOL COUNTY:	
Fairhaven/New Bedford/ Dartmouth/Westport River	Bluefish, Striped bass, Bonito, Shark, Mackerel, Albacore, Pollock

RHODE ISLAND

Of all the states in the Union, Rhode Island is the smallest. It also has one of the shortest coastlines, barely 40 miles in length from point to point in a straight line. When you consider all the bays and inlets, however, this short distance stretches over 400 miles. With Rhode Island's southern exposure to the warm Gulf Stream, which warms coastal waters early and keeps them warm longer into the season, some of New England's finest saltwater fishing is made readily available.

Like fishermen in Massachusetts, Rhode Island anglers take their saltwater fishing seriously. Saltwater enthusiasts outnumber their freshwater counterparts. When fish are "in", the coast becomes a haven, and many hotspots and productive areas are overly sought. Weekends can be especially crowded, although there is plenty of water to go around.

The big four species for inshore fly fishermen in Rhode Island are the striped bass, bonito, bluefish, and mackerel. Again, the fishing seasons for these fish are long, with the following considered prime periods: striped bass—May through December, with some of the big bass taken in the spring and fall; bonito—July through October; bluefish—July through mid-October; mackerel—June through October. There is also excellent fly fishing for pollock, weakfish, shark, and cobia.

AREA	**SPECIES AVAILABLE**
LITTLE COMPTON, TIVERTON, BRISTOL, JOHNSTON, WARWICK, NORTH KINGSTOWN, NARRAGANSETT COUNTIES:	
Sakonnet Bay/Narragansett Bay	Bluefish, Striped bass, Bonito, Mackerel, Weakfish, Cobia, Shark, Albacore

AREA	SPECIES AVAILABLE
NEW SHOREHAM COUNTY:	
Block Island	Bluefish, Striped bass, Bonito, Mackerel, Shark
NARRAGANSETT COUNTY:	
Point Judith	Bluefish, Striped bass, Bonito, Mackerel, Shark, Pollock
KINGSTOWN COUNTY:	
Card Ponds/Green Hill	Bluefish, Striped bass, Bonito, Mackerel, Cobia, Weakfish
CHARLESTOWN COUNTY:	
Quonochontaug	Bluefish, Striped bass, Bonito, Mackerel, Weakfish, Shark
WESTERLY COUNTY:	
Weekapaug/Watch Hill	Mackerel, Bluefish, Striped bass, Bonito, Shark, Pollock, Weakfish, Cobia

CONNECTICUT

Connecticut is another of those small states which makes up for its size in fine saltwater angling. It also has a fairly long coastline, some 250 miles of it, in fact, as the crow flies. The state is fortunate and, indeed, so are its saltwater anglers, for Connecticut forms the northern border of Long Island Sound, which for decades has been considered one of the prime saltwater fishing areas along the entire East Coast. Like neighboring Rhode Island, Connecticut's southern exposure to the Gulf Stream helps keep offshore and inshore water temperatures warm long into the fall, with excellent fishing action possible starting in early June and stretching into December.

Just about any fish species the angler wants will be found off Connecticut. The big four are striped bass, bluefish, bonito, and mackerel, although several other species such as weakfish, cobia, shark, and albacore are readily available. There is also some active shad fishing in the Connecticut, Farmington, and Scantic rivers in the spring, generally in late April, May, and early June. The latter two rivers are tributaries of the Connecticut, located several miles upstream from the sea.

AREA	SPECIES AVAILABLE
New London County:	
Stonington/Thames River	Bluefish, Striped bass, Bonito, Mackerel
Middlesex County:	
Connecticut River	Striped bass, Bluefish, Mackerel, Cobia, Weakfish, Shark, Shad
New Haven County:	
Clinton/Milford	Striped bass, Bluefish, Mackerel, Weakfish, Shark
Fairfield County:	
Stratford/Greenwich	Striped bass, Bluefish, Mackerel, Weakfish, Shark

Chapter 7

WHERE TO GO AND WHO TO CONTACT: *the Mid-Atlantic States including Chesapeake Bay*

Simply put, some of the finest saltwater fly fishing along the East Coast will be found from New York south to Delaware. No matter what the fly fisherman is looking for—species, from the bluefish to spotted sea trout to dolphin–or habitat, from small tidal rivers and streams to the 20,000 square mile Chesapeake Bay, it will be found in this vast and diverse area. The amount of water available is incredible, and the fishing season is longer in these warmer waters than further north along the coast. Good bluefish and striped bass fishing, for example, is possible from April right through December in some areas, longer still in others.

In some ways, angling in this area is a paradox. The Atlantic Coast from New York south to Delaware is one of the most populated and heavily industrialized areas in the country and yet finding an area to fish is not a problem. While certain areas are somewhat more crowded than in New England, other areas are virtually *under*fished except by fly fishermen due to depth, weed cover and other conditions which restrict anglers using other types of gear. Also, many areas are so big (Chesapeake Bay is just one example), that even during the height of the season, fly fishermen can always find an area to cast a line.

Another thing I like about this region is the diversity of game fish available, and the long period of time each year they may be successfully caught on flies. Every species of fish caught in New England plus a few others will be found. In fact, although the bluefish action on a fly rod off Cape Cod in Massachusetts is considered superb, in some areas of New York, the Jersey shore, and Chesapeake Bay it is even better! Depending upon whom you talk to, the same can be said of striped bass and several other species as well.

Along with that, the warmer waters south of New England also host a number of fish not as readily available, or not available at all in Maine, New Hampshire and Massachusetts, for example, thus providing the saltwater fly fisherman with a larger selection of adversaries from which to choose. The dolphin, spotted sea trout, cobia and weakfish are prime examples. Although some of these fish are found in southern New England, the numbers and size of those found from New York south generally far exceed those in waters further north.

And they are available for longer periods of the season, too, as are most other popular saltwater fly fishing game. In Maine, New Hampshire and points north of Cape Cod, the prime fishing months are July and August with some fish showing up in mid-June staying until the middle or later days of September, depending upon water temperatures. In New York, New Jersey and especially areas further south to Chesapeake Bay, however, good action is often available as early as April or early May, with October, November, and even December considered good or prime time for a number of game fish. In layman's terms, fly fishermen in this area are often experiencing *good* action when fishermen further north are gearing up for the annual hunting season or shoveling snow!

The waters in this special area also produce some big fish. The colder waters off New England produce some respectable size saltwater game, but because of the warmer water temperatures and availability of food further south and because certain areas in Chesapeake Bay are important wintering and spawning grounds for a number of saltwater fish, they are able to reach larger lengths and weights in this region. New Jersey has produced world fly fishing record bonito, and Delaware has spawned world fly fishing record weakfish. Along with this, New York has produced world record striped bass, bluefish and pollock, as have New Jersey and Maryland.

So, with everything considered, the waters of New York, New Jersey, Delaware and Maryland have a great deal to offer the saltwater fly fisherman: plenty of area to fish, long fishing seasons, consistent action and large numbers of fish, to say nothing of the possibility of taking a potential world record. It is all here and more. And more and more people are taking advantage of the vast resources readily available, many of them just a short distance away from some of the East Coast's largest metropolitan areas.

Finding a productive spot to fly fish in this area is not a major problem. However, because so much is available, deciding on one particular locale, when to fish it and finding which fish are available can be overwhelming at times, particularly for the enthusiast just starting out. With that in mind, it is important and helpful to remember certain things mentioned in previous chapters.

I have always found it beneficial, for example, to patronize local tackle and bait shops even though they may not have much to offer the fly fisherman along the lines of tackle and gear. The information they can provide is priceless when it comes to suggesting a particular spot, time to fish it, how to get there and what is available. Time and time again I have entered a bait shop somewhere, told the person behind the counter what I am looking for and what I wanted to fish for, piqued his interest, and found he couldn't do enough to help me out. Many have become reliable contacts over the years; I think most fly fishermen will find it is easy to develop a relationship with these shops that can prove to be a great asset. Keep in mind, too, many saltwater bait and tackle shop owners or proprietors are avid fly fishermen themselves. And although their shop may not directly cater to the genre, they may have plenty to say and advice to offer.

Another good source of information in a particular area are charter boat services and guides. Virtually every city, town, village and wide spot in the road from New York to Delaware—especially the larger bays and more popular fishing areas—has at least one or two, and just like bait and tackle shops, they can provide a wealth of information. What is more important, charter services and guides have the means to actually get you on the water, over lots of fish at the right time and show you what to use and how to catch those fish. Such services cost money, of course, but here again, I have always believed using a guide or a charter service at least once is one of the best ways to acquaint oneself with a particular area or method of angling for a particular fish species.

Charter boats generally hire out for $150 to $250 per day, but that cost can be split among the number of fishermen in the group to make it more affordable. Guide rates vary, but generally run from $75 to $125 per day. For some, this may seem like a great deal to invest for a single day's fishing. But what can be discovered and learned that day can last a lifetime. Most state travel bureaus, chambers of commerce, and state departments of natural resources, departments of environmental conservation and fish and wildlife departments, may offer a list of available charter services and guides. The following departments and addresses might be of help:

Delaware Dept. of Natural Resources and
  Environmental Control
Edward Tatnall Building
Dover, DE 19901
Tel: (302) 736-4403

Maryland Dept. of Natural Resources
Towes State Office Building
Annapolis, MD 21401
Tel: (301) 974-3990

New Jersey Dept. of Environmental Protection
Div. of Fish, Game & Shellfisheries
P.O. Box 1809
Trenton, NJ 08625
Tel: (609) 292-9450

New York State Dept. of Environmental Conservation
Building 40–SUNY
Stony Brook, NY 11790
Tel: (516) 751-7900
Tel: (718) 482-4900 (For western Long Island)

New York Outdoor Guides Assoc.
P.O. Box 4337
Albany, NY 12204

Keep in mind, too, national and regional magazines dealing specifically with saltwater angling are another great source of information, even though they may not deal with fly fishing. As mentioned in Chapter 6, two of the very best are *The Fisherman* and *Saltwater Sportsman,* both of which have editions dealing with New York and/or New Jersey, Maryland, Delaware and Chesapeake Bay. *The Fisherman* is published weekly, *Saltwater Sportsman* monthly, and both are oriented directly to the saltwater angler. While neither is directed solely to the fly fisherman, each does touch on the subject from time to time. The biggest value these magazines have to the fly fisherman is providing where-to-go type articles covering specific areas and occasional articles on how to fly fish salt water.

THE FISHERMAN
Long Island/Metro
New York Edition
N.E.F. Publishing Co.
Bridge Street/P.O. Box 1994
Sag Harbor, NY 11963

THE FISHERMAN
New Jersey/Delaware Bay
Edition
339 Herbertsville Road
Brick Town, NJ 08724

SALTWATER SPORTSMAN
184 Lincoln Street
Boston, MA 02111

THE FISHERMAN
Maryland/Virginia Edition
138 Kirkcaldy Drive
Elkton, MD 21921

These magazines also provide another service for saltwater fly fishermen. Both list a great many charter services and guides in the form of advertisements. This is particularly helpful for the novice who may not only not know where to go, but who requires additional assistance. Some bait and tackle shops also advertise, providing even more reliable contacts.

NEW YORK

Nearly all of New York's saltwater fishing takes place on Long Island, reached by ferry from Bayonne, New Jersey; via bridges at several points from New York City; and from Bridgeport, Connecticut (to Port Jefferson, about halfway down the north shore); and New London, Connecticut (to Orient Point on the northeastern tip).

Although Long Island has been considered one of the premier saltwater fishing areas along the northeast coast for decades, the vast majority of anglers use surf-casting, spin-casting and other non-fly-fishing gear to find action. Fly fishing is gaining in popularity, however, and the striped bass, shark, sea bass, bonito, weakfish, mackerel, bluefish and pollock, all of which are available around and off Long Island, are now being taken with bucktails, streamers and poppers.

In the general sense, good fishing will be found just about everywhere. Montauk rates as one of the top striped bass spots, with fish moving into that area in early spring, and action continuing all summer with the peak action traditionally seen from September through November. This is also a top spot for shark fishing offshore with the best fishing seen in late July, August and September. Charter boats will be found in the Montauk area for those interested in shark and other offshore angling.

In Long Island Sound, Manhasset Bay, Glen Cove, Mamaroneck, Little Neck Bay and Flushing are all top fishing spots for a variety of fish, including blues, striped bass, mackerel, weakfish and pollock. Shark is also possible. Fly fishing is available from rock jetties, private boats and charters in each of these areas with good fishing possible as early as May, lasting into late fall.

At Block Island there are some fine fly fishing opportunities, and likewise at Orient Point to the north of Montauk and at Gardiner's Bay. Big striped bass and bluefish are plentiful in all these areas from early spring on, but especially in the fall as they move south again for the winter.

Going west from Orient Point, Southold Bay near Shelter Island is a good area for small-boat fishermen looking for weakfish, snapper blues, sea bass, and the occasional striper, depending upon the season. The months of June, July, August, September and October are all good times. Peconic Bay is a prime spot for weakfish, probably one of the best on the entire island along with Great South Bay. One of the best tactics is to chum with live shrimp and cast with small bucktails, feathered streamers and epoxy flies. Weakfish in this area run up to 3 and 4 pounds, although fish up to 10 pounds have been taken on fly rods in recent years.

The south shore of Long Island is traditionally known as a surf fisherman's paradise, but the many fine beaches in that area also offer some fly fishing from mid-May through November. Specific areas to check out include Atlantic Beach, Long Beach, Fire Island Inlet, Great South Bay, Shinnecock Inlet and the Rockaways. At the extreme western end of Long Island near Jamaica Bay there is some exciting school-fish action on blues and striped bass as early as April. Fly fishermen will find some excellent bluefish casting at Great Kills, north of Raritan Bay and Great Kills Park, reached via Hylan Boulevard between Raritan and Highway 278.

Timing is important when fishing Long Island, as it is elsewhere. Bluefish move into the area from the south in mid-to-late spring and are present right through the summer, but peak again in the fall as the fish, which traveled north along the coast, move south. Blues can be taken inshore and offshore, either by casting and trolling from boats or

(Raychard photo)

casting from shore. Mackerel are available from early spring to early summer, with sea bass fishing good from spring through fall, while the fishing for pollock is good year-round. To save time, it is always best to check with a local charter service, guide, or bait and tackle shop to see what is available.

NEW JERSEY

Despite the fact that it is one of the most industrialized and heavily populated states in the country, New Jersey offers some of the finest saltwater angling to be found anywhere. New Jersey is situated at a point along the eastern shore which receives warm water from the south, which attracts species during the summer months more generally associated with the south Atlantic. Yet during the winter, you can fish for species found in New England. Except for an occasional lull in the action, fishing is possible year-round all along New Jersey's extensive coastline.

Along with that, New Jersey anglers will find a wide selection of saltwater environments from which to choose. The state offers quiet bays, miles of surf and beaches and offshore areas, and there are tidal rivers which are ideal for the fly fisherman. In all, New Jersey offers over 100 tidal rivers where there is some kind of saltwater fishing available.

The three big game fish inshore are the striped bass, bluefish and weakfish. There is some rather exciting night fishing for bass and weakfish with fly rods in such areas as Barnegat Bay, the Mullica Inlet, Atlantic City and Cape May, but any of the islands from Ocean Gate south to Wildwood Crest will provide fishing of this type. Anglers will find good action in these areas during the day, too. It should be remembered that hip boots or chest waders will be required to get through the boggy spots and across small coves and inlets for which the New Jersey shore is famous. Insect repellent is a must during the spring and summer. New Jersey's bogs and marshes are famous for their mosquitos and biting insects.

Traditionally, striped bass reach good numbers in schools along the south Jersey coast in April. Some action will also be found in the Island Beach State Park, Great Egg and Maurice Rivers area, but the fishing is generally deep, calling for large streamers and sinking lines. Sea bass and pollock are available at this time, too, in the same areas. Some of the best action will be had by working from a drifting boat, casting and retrieving.

In May, the striped bass numbers are steadily on the increase and the fishing improves as it does for bluefish, weakfish and pollock. By the time June rolls around, fishing for all species has reached its peak with excellent action continuing right through the summer. In September, the bluefish action is about as good as it gets all year with the later weeks of the month and October considered prime time. The same is true for striped bass. Except for late June and early July, the fishing simply doesn't get any better than in October. Some other good fishing areas include Shrewsbury Rocks, Barnegat Ridge, Sandy Hook and Five Fathom Bank, but keep in mind the fishing is excellent all along the Jersey shore during these early and late seasons. Fly fishing is possible from shore or wading. In a boat, you can drift or anchor and cast. Once a school has been located, you can even troll large streamers and bucktails.

New Jersey also offers excellent offshore fishing, especially for bonito, dolphin, albacore and shark. The best time for these fish appears to be August, September and early October, but don't expect to find action as early as July. In October, the action on large pollock can be unbelievable inshore right along with the action on striped bass, blues and weakfish.

Fortunately, almost every town along the New Jersey shore has a marina with at least one or two charter boats for hire. Notable fleets will be found at Hoboken, Atlantic Beach, Atlantic Highlands, Seabright, Monmouth Beach, Long Beach, Neptune, Brielle, Point Pleasant, Long Beach Island, Barnegat Light, Atlantic City, Ocean City, Avalon, Stone Harbor and Wildwood. Contact with them can usually be made through the local chamber of commerce.

As for other areas where good fishing from shore or small boats is possible, look into the waters near Seabright, Monmouth, Long Branch, Elberon, Deal, Avon-by-the-Sea, Asbury Park, Shark River, Manasquan Inlet, Beach Haven, Brigantine and North Wildwood. Besides the species already mentioned, there is also some exciting fishing for sea trout in many of these areas from July through early October.

Finally, don't overlook the Delaware Bay area. Located at the southernmost tip of the state, Delaware Bay offers top fishing for blues, stripers and weakfish on fly fishing gear with June and September the prime months. Of particular interest to the fly fisherman are the Shrewsbury and Navesink rivers which experience a run of small bluefish running 2 to 5 pounds. The fishing is generally best out of small boats and skiffs in June. The Delaware River also experiences one of the largest runs of anadromous shad although some of the best fishing is not found until you reach Trenton and points further north which are all fresh water. Good shad fishing comes in May and June. Mackerel fishing is excellent along the south Jersey shore, too, particularly for the king mackerel or kingfish in Delaware Bay. These fish reach weights up to 7–25 pounds, although the larger specimens are generally found in deeper water.

DELAWARE

Delaware is a small state covering just over 2,050 square miles. Only Rhode Island covers less area, but some wonderful saltwater fishing is available. The Atlantic Ocean touches only a short stretch of Delaware, basically from Cape Henlopen on the north to Fenwick Island on the south, but with the Delaware River and Bay areas there is plenty of water in which to wet a fly. There are also a number of other rivers and bays along the coast.

As elsewhere along the coast north to New York and New Jersey, bluefish and striped bass are prime targets among saltwater anglers in Delaware. There is good fishing for both just about year-round, although the best fly fishing for these species is in late May and June and again in September and October with good action through the summer. The later months are particularly good for blues, probably the best of the entire year.

Starting in the north, Delaware Bay and the Delaware River upstream to New Castle are good for both striped bass and bluefish, but mostly for blues which make a strong appearance in September after the first cold spell. The Bay is generally shallow which makes it an excellent spot for the fly fisherman working from points, jetties and boats. Boats are usually available for rent in the New Castle area, at Delaware Beach, at Port Penn and Bay View Beach. Charters are also available, which take the angler out not only for stripers and blues but for weakfish, which are available in good numbers and provide excellent fly fishing action, and for king mackerel or kingfish. Some of the best fishing for weakfish and kingfish will be found in Delaware Bay from Bower's Beach south to the open ocean.

There is, however, some excellent fishing for bluefish and striped bass from this point. Striped bass action picks up starting in May and reaches a peak in June. The fall is the best time for bluefish, although both fish are available along the coast in such places as Lewes near Cape Henlopen, accessible via Route 18 from Georgetown, Rehoboth, the next port to the south, Indian River and Indian Bay. Charters and

(Delaware Dept. of Natural Resources and Environmental Control)

guides are available for hire in each of these areas—contact can be made by obtaining names, addresses, and telephone numbers through local chamber of commerce offices or the Delaware Department of Natural Resources and Environmental Control in Dover (see page 154).

From Rehoboth south, the Delaware coast is protected by a strip of islands and sandbars, running for about 10 miles. There is some good striped bass fishing in the surf during the spring and for bluefish in the fall, although the action is not as good as inside Rehoboth Bay, Indian River Bay and Delaware Bay to the north. It is worth investigating, however, if the fly fisherman hits it at the right time.

Offshore, Delaware fishermen can take advantage of several species besides striped bass and bluefish, which are also found in deep water. These species are augmented by an occasional dolphin, and good action on bonito, albacore and other small tuna. Delaware also offers some active fishing for mackerel which are always a joy on light fly-fishing gear.

Remember, too, the Delaware is a prime shad fishing river, with fair to good action possible upstream to Wilmington, although shad fishing in this state is nowhere as good as it is in Pennsylvania and New York on the same river.

MARYLAND

From the Susquehanna River in its northeast corner to the Potomac along its southern border to Chesapeake Bay's 20,000 square miles and all the rivers flowing into it, Maryland without question offers the angler some of the finest saltwater fishing along the entire East Coast. Just about any species the fly fisherman is looking for is here, including striped bass—Chesapeake Bay and its tributaries are major spawning and wintering grounds for this fish—bluefish, mackerel, cobia, sea trout, kingfish, shark, bonito, dolphin, albacore, wahoo and two species of shad. The list is impressive and the angling, which is available year-round, is, also.

Because Maryland has so much to offer and the areas are so big, it might be best to take a close look at specific spots and learn what they have to offer. Obviously, not all saltwater fishing areas available can be mentioned, but these which are will get the fly fisherman started in this unique and productive area.

TIDEWATER/ESTUARY AREAS

Some of the best fly fishing in Maryland will be found in tidewater and saltwater estuary areas surrounding Chesapeake Bay. When put together, they total some 5,000 square miles of top fishing grounds, most of which offer a wide array of game fish and are relatively easy to find and reach.

The Susquehanna River, for example, is considered one of the premier striped bass fishing spots along the East Coast. There is good bass fishing upstream to the dam and at Susquehanna Flats at the mouth of the river. There are about 4 miles of river in this section with bass traditionally moving into the area around the end of May, remaining until mid-October or later. This is a great fly-fishing stretch of water offering relatively consistent action all season long. Bucktails and streamers tied on large 1/0 and 3/0 size hooks in red/white, yellow/red and white/black or brown are popular. The Gibbs Striper Fly, Lefty's Deceiver, Honey Blonde and Platinum Blonde are favorite patterns among local fishermen. Popping bugs in the same color schemes do well, too. There is nothing quite like having a good sized striped bass rise and wallop a popper, and this is one of the best areas in Maryland to try it!

Shad also run up the Susquehanna—both the hickory and American versions. Hickories start showing up in early April with good fishing continuing until July. The American shad arrive in mid-May traditionally providing action into the middle or later part of June. Fly fishermen should look for these scrappy individuals in riffles and glides, with the hickory shad typically preferring slightly slower water. Small white, fluorescent red and fluorescent pink flies tied on gold hooks, sizes 6, 8 and 10 are excellent. Keep in mind the key to success is getting the fly down, so weighted flies tied to short leaders and sinking lines might be helpful.

South of the Susquehanna River and entering Chesapeake Bay on the west shore, the Patuxent River offers many miles of fine water. The river has stripers, bluefish and sea trout starting as early as May with fish and good fly fishing available well into October. Boats and guides will be found at California on Route 235, at Benedict and at Solomons. Some of the best fishing will be found on the Patuxent's lower stretches, mostly those areas close to Chesapeake Bay.

The Potomac is another top river. There is seasonal fishing for shad in May and June and striped bass will be found throughout all the way to Washington, D.C. Some of the best striper action will be found where Route 301 crosses the Potomac downstream to the bay and at the mouth of smaller tributaries. Here again, May, June and September and October are traditionally top months but action is possible all summer long.

Gibbs Striper Fly (Raychard photo)

The closer the fisherman gets to the bay, the better the fishing gets on the Potomac—some of Chesapeake Bay's best cobia fishing will be found near Wayne in August to late October where boats and a few guides will be found. Smith Creek, near the town of Wayne, is a good spot for striped bass. Another good tributary of the Potomac in this area is the Port Tobacco River which offers shad in season.

Other good rivers entering the bay include the Magothy—reached by Route 2 from Baltimore—which offers striped bass in the spring and fall. The Severn and South rivers, both easily reached from Washington, D.C. via U.S. Routes 50 and 301 and from Baltimore via Routes 2 and 3, both offer occasional runs of stripers in the spring and fall, too.

THE EASTERN SHORE

Separating Chesapeake Bay from southern Delaware and the Atlantic Ocean is a strip of land known as the Delmarva Peninsula. Among the locals and fishermen familiar with the area this section of Maryland is called the "Eastern Shore" and to most it represents some of the finest and most exciting fishing Chesapeake Bay has to offer.

Several rivers are found on this side of the bay. About halfway down the Choptank River, which enters the bay at Cambridge, is a good place for striped bass. The best action is generally found in May, from Cook Point near the mouth upstream to about where Route 50 crosses the river. Good action continues into June or when warm weather sets in pushing the fish into the cooler waters of the bay. There is another run of small stripers in the fall. Bass remain in the river through December—the best fishing at this time is by trolling.

Further down the shore the Nanticoke, Wicomico and Manokin rivers all flow into smaller Tangier Sound, traditionally one of the most popular and productive areas in or around Chesapeake Bay. All species are available including blues, striped bass, mackerel plus a few others when in season, but it is particularly good for sea trout from mid-July through the fall. Another good river is the Pocomoke, which enters Pocomoke Sound on the Virginia border. It is easily reached from Route 113 which happens to parallel the length of the river. Striped bass and shad enter the river and travel upstream as far as Pocomoke City on their seasonal migration, with the best fishing found near the mouth. An occasional bluefish will be taken on the Pocomoke as well.

CHESAPEAKE BAY

While some of the best fly-fishing action for various saltwater game fish will be found in tributary rivers, Chesapeake Bay itself has a great deal to offer the angler who enjoys working from boats, points and jetties. The number of available areas where literally every species of

(Raychard photo)

fish that enters the bay can be taken is impressive. And the angler could spend years exploring and fishing new water each time out.

For starters, however, the following areas will prove most interesting. On the northern end of the bay, look into the Chesapeake Bay Bridge area, Turkey Point, Spesutie Island, Battery Point, Pooles Island, Worton Point, Tea Kettle Shoals, Eastern Neck Island, Hickory Thicket and Love Point. In the southern section of the bay, Dolly's Lumps, Brick House Bar, Bloody Point, Dastern Bay, Poplar Island, Holland Point and Tilghman Island are good. Still further south, Sharps Island, Winter Goose, the James Island area, Round Ragged Point, Little Choptank River, Taylor's Island and Cove Point should be considered. Most charter boat operators and guides are intimately familiar with these spots as are local bait and tackle shops and most will provide information on how to find them, and when and how best to fish them and what is available at a particular time or season.

ATLANTIC SHORE FISHING

Maryland has only about 40 miles of Atlantic coastline but what it does have boils down to some of the best inshore angling on the East Coast. Striped bass invade the waters of Ocean City and the entire length of Assateague Island on their journey northward in May and June and again in September through October as they head south. Stripers are often found very close to shore hugging the shoals and although the surf is not the ideal environment for the fly rod, on calm spring days it is possible to reach them by wading or from small boats and skiffs traveling parallel with the coast just outside the breakers.

In mid-summer, anglers will find bluefish, sea trout, small kingfish and mackerel and, of course, striped bass throughout the area. To reach Assateague Island, fishermen must either rent a boat at Ocean City at the end of U.S. Route 50, take a ferry from South Point, or travel from the Virginia side from Chincoteague via Route 13 and State Highway 175.

Other top fishing areas along the Atlantic coast other than Assateague Island include the jetties at the mouth of the Sinepuxent Bay and Sinepuxent Bay itself. The smaller bays in this area are excellent for sea trout, bluefish and striped bass. Other species show up from time to time as well.

OFFSHORE FISHING

Much of the offshore fishing in Maryland starts off at Ocean City, where boats by the dozen and guides are available. Open water species include dolphin, bonito, albacore, kingfish, bluefish, striped bass, mackerel and wahoo. All are available starting in June, remaining until September and October, if not later.

The Illustrator

Rock J. Agostino was born in Massachusetts and moved to Maine in 1976. He is a 1978 graduate of Unity (Maine) College, with a degree in Wildlife Fisheries Science. The following year he founded Creative Maine Taxidermy, Inc., in Kennebunk, Maine, a business which he now owns in partnership with Anne Gorham. He holds the Carl Akeley Medallion, awarded in an international taxidermy competition in 1985.

Notes

Notes

Notes